WINDING DOWN AND SELLING OUT THE UNITED STATES
THE COURSE OF AN HISTORICAL SELF-DESTRUCT

WINDING DOWN AND SELLING OUT THE UNITED STATES

THE COURSE OF AN HISTORICAL SELF-DESTRUCT

By

FRED K. VIGMAN

Author of The Fateful Subversion of the American Economy **etc.**

THE CHRISTOPHER PUBLISHING HOUSE
NORTH QUINCY, MASSACHUSETTS 02171

COPYRIGHT © 1973
BY THE CHRISTOPHER PUBLISHING HOUSE
Library of Congress Catalog Card Number 73-79084
ISBN: 1−8158−0308−7

PRINTED IN
THE UNITED STATES OF AMERICA

For
JOHN LUKACS
the historian for these parlous times

CONTENTS

A Self-Review by Way of Preface.............. 7
Introduction 15
    Distorting Mirrors to Ward Off Facing
        the Head of Medusa
    A Game Plan for Doomsday Might Help
I. Preparing for Armageddon the Hosts Create
    Its Inevitability 21
II. The Spanish Curse, or the Two-Way Sell-Out
    of the United States 29
III. Wind-Down of Domestic Industries 41
    Steel: The Undergird Buckling Badly
    Textiles: Foreign Imports Are Its
        Winding Sheet
    Clothing: Another Industry Being
        Stitched a Shroud
    Electronics: Yankee Ingenuity Short-Circuited
IV. Services and Governmental Outstrip the Productive—Living by Taking in Each Other's Wash .. 53
V. Obsolescent U.S.A.—Or Industrial Might
    Undermined by the Righteous 61
    Dead Capital Meet Dead Labor or Phasing
        Out an Industrial Order
    Railroads: Scraping the Roads of Destiny
    The New Cabal—Automobiles, Oil and
        the Highway Behemoth

8   Winding Down and Selling Out the United States

> *The Structurally Unemployed: A New*
> *Estate of the Welfare State*
> *The Patriots Depart These Shores in*
> *Self-Righteous Hypocrisy*
> *Closing in on the Premier Secondary*
> *Domestic Firms*

VI. All Moneyed Hands Plan to Abandon Ship ... 84
VII. The Economists as Yes-Sayers and Dutiful
  Pollyannas—and Fools to Boot............ 89
  Glossing the Breakup of the World
  Monetary System
VIII. Inflation Built in by the Parasitism of the M-I
  Complex and the Obsolescence of Commodity Production 105
  Lo the Dying Stock Market—The Drying
  Up of Public Capital
IX. Taxes: The Classic Trick That Turned the
  Tide to Disaster 117
  Tax Revolts: Too Little and Too Late
X. U.S. in Receivership—President Nixon, the
  Flexible Apocalypist, Hardly the Proper
  Receiver............................ 127
  Labor: The Last Defender of the Faith
  The New Economic Policy: The Economics
  of a Purported New Start
  The Dollar Rout and Monetary Rot
XI. In Meantime Back at the Pentagon the M-I
  Complex Demands Its Annual Lion's
  Share and Gets It 139
  The Loss Leader Persists in Its Claim as
  Savior While Increment Goes Down the

The Course of an Historical Self-Destruct 9

> *Drain and Foreign Capital Moves to
Take Over
The Trojan Horse Wheedled in by Urging
of Beleaguered U.S.
All Eyes Look to the Rising Sun of Japan
Now That It Has Set in the U.S.
The Erstwhile Enemies Alone Offer
Succour to a Foundering U.S.*

XII. U.S. in Its Fall Persists in Dragging World
into a Vast Crisis 155
XIII. Boom's End: Professor Webb's Paradigm of
American Destiny 159
> *The Prophecies of Doom: A Sense of
Historical Realities*

XIV. The Final Read-Out—the Immolation of a
Self-Consuming Society 167

A Brief Bibliography 175
Appendix I, Projected Deficits 1973-1979 ... 177
Appendix II, The Depletion of New England
and Middle Atlantic Industries 179
Appendix III, Newspapers Threatened by
Urban Crisis 183
Index 187

A SELF-REVIEW BY WAY OF PREFACE

Anthony Burgess, the popular British novelist now immured in Italy, revealed an old truth. "The fairest review that any novel of mine ever received was one I wrote myself. At least I read the book and knew it pretty thoroughly, so I was able to discuss its faults and virtues with some confidence." The usual and accepted form of a self-review is an abstract. I find it too limited for my purposes. I couched it in the guise of a critical but sympathetic historian making a go at it, giving him my insights (a neat trick, but one that will raise eyebrows and bring on frowns from the academics). What is patent is that it is addressed to the historians. But to be fair, professional historians have limited areas and stakes in historiography. They have narrow competences and dare not poach on one another and certainly not venture into the wide sweep of Gibbonian terrain. I would pray that Toynbee would include the matter to crown his efforts to get at the decline and fall of empires.

Given academic preoccupation and occupational sensitivity the historian sniffs the air for a clue. By tone and treatment the present study is hardly more than an extended editorial. It does not follow the prescribed format of academic historicism in defining terms, noting the extant literature and comparative studies, the models of facts and figures. In short it does not have the formidable *apparat* which is the trademark of the discipline. Very well, testing it as journalism we can hold it to be skimpy, disjecta, such as marks the newspaper's readers own historical awareness.

But then—and this will reveal the chink in the historian's armor—the meager materia is prolegomena of a new historical awareness which would take hundreds of studies or books to give it a familiar status. We can agree with the notion that it is a workbook, a code book, to get the brethren unto the historical mainstream. The snippet sub-sections could be the *point d'appui* for endless studies. The work then, to give it premature hubris, is seminal.

There does emerge an historiographic schema. Vigman relies on academic historicism and gives pride of place to the late Professor Walter Webb. It would indicate that we academicians have failed to follow up on Webb's awareness. There were no studies of his theorems after his death, yet he gave us the only viable paradigm, now that the Frontier and Manifest Destiny coda have come to the water's edge and fallen in.

It would appear that our author hardly fleshes out the Webb theorem, even if he calls attention to it. We could wish that it would be done in a 700-page work, the salient mark of the academic modus. Perhaps we should be grateful that a non-academic was daring enough to start the trend. He calls attention to the Webb paradigm as the new start in American historical consciousness, a phase of my favorite theme. Further, that we are working within the area of the presumptive

The Course of an Historical Self-Destruct   13

decline and fall of the American Empire, to give it a classical turn. Vigman is no Gibbon; he is not the unhurried chronicler after the event but the harried courier hurrying to bear the tidings of defeat, for which he may be stoned or ignored.

The paradox of contemporary political life is the refusal—stubborn and unremitting—to acknowledge historical reality. I make much of historical consciousness and its growth (see Lukac's *History of Consciousness: or the Remembered Past*) and this gives me pause. Postwar America was suspended in the fearful void of the atomic apocalypse. Tracing our author's clues the great change for disaster occurred without any marked awareness of the massive shift. A war-and-war materiel prosperity was enough for the day's travail for the humble folk.

Winding Down etc. is a sustained *explanas* if we refer to it as a sequel to *The Fateful Subversion of the American Economy, Consequent on the Gold/Dollar, Trade/ Economic and Tax Crises* (there's an eighteenth century title, but it covers the ground). That work was a discovery or illumination of a new and strange era of the breakdown of modern society. To his credit and sense of historical reality Vigman traced the steps of the breakup of what he termed the normative commodities order, the free enterprise system (purportedly dear to the Chamber of Commerce and the loyal legion of labor) the bourgeois order which the educated saw as the fulfillment of history.

As Vigman found out, none would admit it, much less accept it, even for argument or to disprove. The academicians, moreso the economists and the government which engineered the great coup and is now referee in bankruptcy, bent all efforts to prove that the U. S. was in the midst of a virulent boom. Indeed it was a boom, the penultimate frenzy of automobile production, a desperate world-wide search for oil and billions for highways (the unholy trinity of the debased economy). It is a *Todentanz*. It is our bourgeois world (an idealized version which Vigman and I value) being ground to bits.

The new, unprecedented conditions, the *terra incognita* of the disintegrating normative economic order, make all antecedent historical modes redundant. Keeping speculation under restraint it may be said that it reduces previous history to antiquarianism. Historiography needs a basic reorientation. Our academicians refuse to recognize it. In point of fact there is now a mad rush to get at it, the swing to a refurbished Marxism the most visible. The older academicians draw comparisons, rather abstractly and obliquely, with past empires which have foundered.

All disciplines, so finely honed, are now superannuated because they were based on the social-political conditions of the old commodities society so cruelly done in. All variants of Marxism, presumably the revolutionary position, are in a like fix. At this date the tenets of Marxism are in question: the proletariat have been in front ranks of the *condottiere* who wrecked the normative commodities order which they were to inherit and to raise to a more orderly progression. The suspicion is growing that the peasantry have been the background, meaning and force behind all revolutionary reorganizations from the French Revolution onward.

— *F. K. V.*

INTRODUCTION
DISTORTING MIRRORS TO WARD OFF FACING THE HEAD OF MEDUSA

There had been any number of pastiche Medusae in American history in the guise of grinning skeletons—cheerful, hopeful Death's Heads, markers of the onward and upward reach of American Destiny. Even the Apocalypse with the four horsemen transposed to aircraft carrying the atom bomb with its threat (or promise) of instant annihilation, was taken in stride because it was the evangelical mythology protected by an ostensibly affluent society. But in the offing, and offstage, was the Medusa with her ringlets of writhing serpents—the wind-down and subversion of the economic order to a new and strange economic system—could not be faced head-on. When it was approached it was fearfully glimpsed in distorting mirrors.

The economists—academic, governmental and private businessmen and bankers—had, by the opening of 1971, become the exigent high priests. On every notch or escalation of the monetary and corollary economic crises the economists were rushed into the breach before and after the event. The weekly news magazines had their soothsayers and not to get caught, had a team or called in a collegium for summary conclusions and forecasts. What was lacking in the dense thicket of arguments was the mention of the fate of similar economists who had plied their search of the entrails before and after the Great Depression of the 1930s. They had been too Canutean in their determinations and were hopelessly compromised, dismissed and forgotten in the ensuing New Deal economics. The present generation of economists were headed for the same ignominy. But there arose a skepticism abroad, that indicated that the petitioners, waiting below, carried in their memory, but would not acknowledge that the high priests were not to be believed, although all wanted to desperately. *The New York Times,* now the leading organ of the internationalists, that is, the bankers and industrialists who would break national bonds to tranplant their businesses to Europe and other parts and open up the country to foreign trade and exploitation, had more than its share of economic writers, obfuscators all. There was enough sophistication in their ranks to realize that they were hardly more than second-guessers and, consequently, they let through an occasional self-caricature. One such was a piece by Robert D. Hershey, Jr., and the copyreader who wrote the heads, did it justice. "Oracles Play a Precarious Trade. Economic Forecasts (Even if Official) Lack Guarantee." Even more revealing was the sketch (an innovative idea for the *Times*) accompanying the piece. At the left was a box "Astrological Study" with two zodiac symbols, then an open palm representing palmistry labeled "Business Forecast." The zodiac box and palm funneled into a computer "Business Forecast Computer." To the left of the Rube Goldberg computer was the White House with a large question mark hover-

The Course of an Historical Self-Destruct

ing over it and to the left an ear apparently listening for an echo. "The year just concluded was generally quite successful for the business prophets, but they were helped considerably by the Administration's control program begun in mid-August.... For the most part, and not surprisingly, the predictions made by the business community — whether by individuals, institutions or professional groups — fared better than those of the Federal Government, which had an exceptionally poor year. ...Forecasters have long had an unsavory reputation in some quarters and those who take them seriously should be aware that they operate with total disregard of the possible legal consequences of their exercises" (February 1, 1972). The whole business of forecasting was based on a false premise and a false model—that of the Gross National Product—which was a messy clot in which monies of seventy-five percent of the working force was parasitic (services, government, war, etc.) while only twenty-five percent of all income was from the productive sector, lumped together as gross national income. It was essentially a distorting-mirror, hence a fraud.

Some economists, in desperation, sought to break through the self-imposed model insisted on by the official and para-official, following the disingenuous line of the Administration. Professor Edwin Mansfield, professor of economics at the Wharton School of the University of Pennsylvania, in assaying the "Contribution of R & D to Economic Growth in the United States," admitted, "that much of the nation's R & D is devoted to defense and space purposes. For example, some observers note the tremendous increase in expenditures on R & D in the postwar period and conclude that, because productivity has not risen much faster in this period than it did before the war, the effect of R & D on economic growth must be very small. What these observers forget is that the bulk of the nation's expenditures on R & D has been devoted to defense and space objectives and that the contribution of such expenditures to economic growth may have been limited." The professor and other economists know the answer: the $500 billion spent on R & D (Research and Development) applied only to arms and weapon systems. It did not affect productive commodity industry, which on the contrary, lost out because of the growing obsolescence and deterioration of equipment (the Italian Olivetti people were amazed at the shabby factory they possessed in taking over the Remington typewriter operations): textiles, shoes, and steel techniques falling behind that of foreign countries. The preponderance of R & D funds for war products should have been objective evidence of a pattern. Mansfield admitted as much: "The relevance to economic growth of much of his huge investment in defense and space R & D, has been questioned by many economists." But like the brethren of the "upswing-wing," the economists never followed up such doubts, or even drew back. They sensed what was at the end of the tunnel.

A GAME PLAN FOR DOOMSDAY MIGHT HELP

The economists and self-serving Administrative officials worked hard and tediously to give the offending

The Course of an Historical Self-Destruct

economic crisis the respectable and acceptable facade of a recession. They were as one, with those who are not ready to face up to historic facts. On the contrary, there was a drawing together to keep alive those gruesome myths of the apocalyptic base: that we were living in a new highpoint technological order. They regarded the various crises as the process of sloughing off the old economic order. The Europeans gasped at the indifference, even *sang froid* of a people who accepted what would drive a normative people mad with despair. But the game was played grimly through to the end although the events of the day would prove otherwise. The phantasmagorgia of war games was now elided into game plans. The people were as one with the doers-and-shakers, although here and there, alienated persons believed they saw through the fearsome charade.

Behind the glitter of chrome, the vastness of huge skyscrapers and millions of automobiles, and behind all the sleekness of huge airplanes, civil and military, the United States had been reduced to a gargantuan parasitic society, living off itself and its own past industriousness. It was busy cannabalizing itself. For the most part, commodity, industry and family farming was phased out; the grounds of livelihood had been undercut. The greater part of the population on the wage rolls were supernumaries living off the confiscatory taxes of the still gainfully employed. All efforts of the government as Administrator of the bankrupt country were directed to finding ever new sources of money and taxes. Each turn of the screw narrowed the field of operation. History foreclosed on the richest, greatest, etc. country ever. The surviving generation would have no alternative but to start from scratch or sink, much like the older Asiatic societies, into the mire.

The post-war Doomsday sayers were given proper attention, accorded solemn reviews and admired as responsible citizens. Paradoxically the apocalypse-prone refused to face up to the Gorgon when it was brought too close to them. They were willing to bow resignedly to a distant doom of large, vast, impersonal forces, but withdrew in horror from one, close-up, which affected and touched their daily lives.

All of the above is by way of introduction to the reception given *The Fateful Subversion of the American Economy, Consequent on the Gold/Dollar, Trade/Economic and Tax Crises* (1971). This was not the severed head of Medusa but the living Fate herself. No one could face her because they felt her in their bones. It indicated a loss of nerve, a jangled fear of the onrushing terror.

I. PREPARING FOR ARMAGEDDON THE HOSTS CREATE ITS INEVITABILITY

Apocalypse, congenial to the American evangelical strain, was first glimpsed in the Great Depression of the 1930s. It became the official doctrine of the postwar years and a fateful revanche was mounted for the Final Judgment on a world-wide battlefield. Using this as the pretext, the economy on which all was based was fatefully compromised. A hard-driving private enterprise system, even though it destroyed resources, was, in the Western tradition converted to a non-commodity arms and weapons economy, undercutting the historic economic order.

Cast adrift in new and strange historical conditions, the pretext was maintained that all was conventionally right given the overhang of the final Götterdämmerung of the forces of good and evil. In this circumstance the vast destruction of the accumulated capital of generations, some ten trillion, was accepted as the price and cheap enough at that. Consolation was awarded by a frenetic prosperity, created by such gargantuan expenditures in a comparatively short time. Basically it was an historic self-destruct.

In the self-conscious 1950s there was a dominant political mood that was apocalyptic in putting the future in terms of survival, in a clash with the Communist world. Under the dictum of metaphysics popular then, there were two diametrically opposed views of America's rendezvous with destiny. Neither view was defined by historians so much, as by publicists, business tycoons, economists and scientists. Historians were rather shy of forecasting the future, although in Professor Walter Prescott Webb's Great Frontier thesis there was a most persuasive hypothesis for an insight into the rise and fall of American Destiny.

The first school—the boom enthusiasts—were not nearly as solid a phalanx as "the prophets of doom," as Professor Marston Bates termed them, but the former represented the prevalent apocalyptic view and mood. They thought in terms of a "fabulous" future, with the horn of plenty dumping its products in ever greater profusion. Morris L. Ernst who saw it as *Utopia 1976,* believed that the outpouring would come because of "new sources of energy" and the "chemical revolution on our farms." With the masses now the possessors of "vast new leisure" they could live it up with an average income of $25,000 per year per family. The editors of *Fortune,* in their view of the "fabulous future," were more modest, alloting "for the average family unit a 1980 spending income in excess of $8,000" based on a fifty percent increase in the rate of productivity. And top *Time* economist Henry C. Luce wrote that "abundance has become visibly the norm of life in America. Having been achieved in America as a human reality, this economy of abundance is likely to become the global condition of man's life on earth."

In a more rational and less hyperbolic approach, several writers, while not holding the future to be fabulous, were ready to contest the prophets of doom. A. G. Mezerik in *The Pursuit of Plenty* held that if there was control and husbanding of natural resources the growing pressure on these could be contained. Moreover, these resources could be renewed through conversion of wood into sugar, sea algae into food, desalted salt water for irrigation. In a like vein, Michael W. Straus, a one time assistant to Secretary of the Interior, Harold L. Ickes, averred in *Why Not Survive?*, "we have the natural resources on which to survive with a constantly improving standard of living— if we are willing to use them wisely." Going out on a century-long limb, Harrison Brown, James Bonner and John Weir in *The Next Hundred Years* professed to be optimistic even at the prospect of a seven billion world population. They saw the United States holding its lead position and for resources they would have recourse to the scientific ingenuity of the times.

The scientists who felt they were called on to save the materiél civilization against the threats to it, came up with their horrendous future, less fabulous, that envisaged warehouses with algae from the good seas. Paul B. Sears, then president of the American Association for the Advancement of Science depicted the surrealist nightmare. "What if the space on earth is finite? Homes can be built in stacks and men made to like it. What if the supply of fossil fuel has its limits and is being used recklessly. We have tapped the atom and shall tap the sun direct. When metallic ores become dissipated we shall grind up granite and pump out the sea to extract the materials we need. When food from shrinking and impoverished fields becomes scarce enough, we shall make food. We shall find substitutes for dwindling materials, and substitutes for substitutes, world without end." A searing prophecy.

Such disparate estimates, at first glance irreconcilable, were two sides of the same coin. The first school watched the rising productive curve on the national graph and based all their estimates on it. The second group saw the rise but as a portent of disaster, inasmuch as it was the final terminal point in mining the resources of the continent with a greater population pressing for its final cleanup.

Then, too, there were the scientist-educators who saw catastrophe hang over industrial civilization because, Frankenstein-like technology has become a means of wholesale destruction of nature. Dr. Karl T. Compton, president of the Massachusetts Institute of Technology, warned the graduating class of 1948 that unless the process be checked and natural resources be conserved there was "an impending danger of catastrophe. More and more the reserves of our country are being exhausted. It is estimated that about one-third of our original fertility has been lost by erosion. We are told the world supply of lead would be exhausted within ten or eleven years at the present rate. Oil and iron reserves have been increasingly matters of serious concern. These are long range problems but if we look to the future of our children and grandchildren the problems loom very large indeed."

The mastery of nature, that oft repeated boast, was basically a self-delusion. Dr. Vannevar Bush, president of the Carnegie Institution of Washington, warned in his retiring report in 1955 that industrial man was headed for "catastrophe unless he mends his ways." The basic resources of industrialization were being eaten up at an "appalling rate," with vast new populations called into being as markets for industrial products, depending more heavily on greater production.

Dr. George T. Kimble, director of the American Geographical Society warned in 1952 that a reversal was in order, that industrial man better learn to "pull in his belt" and learn to live within the means offered by his environment, "which was now an economy of scarcity." In what was a warning against the mania for industrialization now stirring other sections of the world he held that "if the world's steel output were to rise to the per capita level of the United States, the world's known iron ore deposits would be exhausted in twenty years, and if the copper output of the world were to rise to the American level all known copper resources would not last more than six years."

Dr. Clifford C. Furnas, chancellor of the University of Chicago, speaking before the 1957 meeting of the American Society of Civil Engineers, held that American industrialization was up a blind alley of depleted resources. The insoluble contradiction of industrial society was that when the underlying resources for industry were running low the pressure for more was mounting in geometric progression. American industrial civilization had been living "high off the hog."

The dominant political mood in the post-war period was apocalyptic—but the question of the future in terms of survival, was envisioned as a putative clash with the Communist world rather than a struggle to overcome depleted resources. The cold war designated the polarity of interests in the world, and made the official governmental line.

Following the perspectives, rules and the bureaucratic creation of the Cold War (1948), the ensuing elán, drive and furious economic activity had concentric circles of apocalyptic frenzy—ever new wonders of atomic terror, arms systems and space exploration. There were wonders to read about and see, but the prevailing current was that the world was girding for Armageddon. The science wonders and arms self-terrorization suited the evangelical (indeed the political theory was that of the evangelicals). For the more literate and liberal of the upper middle class, however, it has a surrealist quality although they were not loath to add their mite to the anti-Communist *hajjah*.

Amid these circumstances the few remaining rationalists felt uneasy. They could not pierce the meaning of the new economic order which they took as an extension of the old; but, President Eisenhower, clear-minded and simple, saw it as the military-industrial complex. It was the grounds for heart-searching after the fashion of intellectuals. As Philip Green, then an instructor in political science, Princeton University wrote: (1961) "The uneasiness over the state of American society, that is today felt in almost every quarter, was first given expression by Adlai Stevenson and George Kennan and then in J. K. Galbraith's *The Affluent Society*. The excited discussion which followed upon *The Affluent Society* (and the reports by the Rockefeller Brothers and the Gaither Committee) became, in 1960, an extended public debate. The symposium on 'National Purpose' sponsored jointly by the *New York Times* and *Life Magazine,* the Report of the President's Commission on National Goals (a token of Eisenhower's recognition of the disintegration around him), and the campaign addresses of John F. Kennedy as well as occasional speeches by Stevenson, Nelson Rockefeller, and once or twice even Richard Nixon)." But such political thinking could not garner much except to call for more effort and discipline in besting the devil incarnate, USSR, fobbed off as Russia. "Despite their forthright tone, however, none of the persons or groups that carried on the 'Great Debate' really has a searching analysis to make of American society; they are merely uneasy and occasionally waspish, and they tend to look at all questions in terms of immediate (and superficial) cold war gains."

Green picked Hans J. Morgenthau, the emigre professor, as a possible source of wider experience (European) and a more acute sense of history. His findings, Green held was "that the American people in the mass today lack any sense of common responsibility for the organization and improvement of their society." The Morgenthau criticism was that of any European intellect who found the social-political situation inchoate, with the familiar landmarks of class and political parties missing, and the lead element, the business-financial, incoherent and atavistic in pursuing their game. There was no one within the confines of the shakers-and-doers to state their position if it needed stating, to push ahead and clean up. Green had only failure to report. "Indeed, despite the intentions of men like Morgenthau, Stevenson, and (Archibald) MacLeish, the only practical meaning that can be given to 'national purpose' under the circumstances I have been describing is a disciplined, crisis-oriented permanent cold war mobilization, beyond which, as Eisenhower said in his farewell address, lies the garrison state."

II. THE SPANISH CURSE, OR THE TWO-WAY SELL-OUT OF THE UNITED STATES

The Spanish Curse that lay athwart the New World since its discovery, and worked its evil for nearly 500 years in plundering and ravaging Latin America, was now on the United States. There was a tragic historical failure to perceive that the economics of the New World were not in kind and effect, that of the Old World (Europe). The exceptionalism was especially marked in Latin America. Its discovery and settlement by the Iberians, a caudillo people with a heavy Oriental underlay which marked them as cruel, patrocentric and exploitative, was fatal for the southern continent. They gutted it of its transportable treasures, killed off millions and reduced the remaining natives to peons, a pattern which was to continue despite the changes wrought by their independence from Spain. Whatever was democratically modern came from the later migrants, the Continental Europeans and the use of European capital. But the Spanish Curse prevailed—almost all the new wealth and increment was garnered by the older, and the parvenu elements, sequestered in European capitals to which they fled and eventually retired.

The plunder of the Americas was the making of Europe and opened up the modern era. The hoards of gold and silver, most of it acquired by the Spanish, and subsequently transferred to the English and Dutch by warfare and piracy, laid the basis for world-wide commerce and established a stable money system. The Atlantic European nations did not believe that the Western Hemisphere was not for their benefit even after the latter countries gained their independence. It was a source of investment and an escape hatch for the millions of their pauperized surplus population.

It would seem academic to argue—and the academics were adept at it—in favor of the startling fact that the viable industries were gathering their resources to decamp the United States as a played-out economic territory and betake themselves to the older and newer countries for profitable operation. It could be seen as a sell-out on such an historic scale and dimension without precedent in history. But it would be presented as the dynamic urge of American industry and business— not content with playing on old overplowed and harrowed fields. It was an extension of the cosmopolitan might of modern industry and then it would prove that the world was really one and the doers-and-shakers would not be tied down to local parishes.

In point of fact it would be a sellout of tremendous and even epic proportions. It would prove far too clearly that the corporation men had no basic loyalty, and would perhaps, regretfully, permit the homestead to be reduced to a Continental Appalachia. "That's the way the ball bounces," which pleads the irreversi-

The Course of an Historical Self-Destruct

bility of historical trends. But they did not propose to leave the locals reduced to penury without some compensation. Falling back on the liberal notion of free trade and free access, they would welcome and even insist and maneuver foreign capital to try a second-strike exploitation of territory they had abandoned. It would be of help to the old folks at home. No shame in having foreigners work-over the old plantation, better than all being on welfare if such be around at that time.

Professor Robert L. Heilbroner, an economist of parts (but more importantly one with several crucial parts missing) did not do well in his piece on "The Multinational Corporation and the Nation-State" (1971). He had the facts but he could not get at their historical significance. Rather he elided the patent conclusion. Heilbroner held that not all corporations were multinational (that is, had foreign operations). "But we do know that sixty-two of the top one hundred firms have production facilities in at least six foreign countries, and Kenneth Simmonds has shown that seventy-one of the top 126 industrial corporations (for which data could be obtained) averaged one-third of their employment abroad." Heilbroner argued that it was an underestimate "but we will have to await the 1970 census data to be sure." Using 1966 data Heilbroner asserted that the United States exported $3 billion in goods and services from the homeland as against $110 billion exports from U. S.-owned factories and plants abroad, the foreign U. S. production being "two and a half times as much."

The big conglomerates built from the ill-gotten monies which were siphoned off the vast tax-monies of the arms industries, were busy packing up. The easy-money tax-way phase was over; now, they would invest in honest but profitable commodity production and that was outside the United States. Gulf and Western Industries, Inc., which had only piddling interests abroad, a decade ago, was ready by June 1971 for major expansion overseas. "We believe our overseas operations represent a major growth area for Gulf and Western in the decade of the seventies and beyond. It is our initial goal to more than triple our international sales to more than $500-million a year by 1976." The overseas operation was termed Gulf and Western International with headquarters in Rome, managing plants in Great Britain, Italy and France and Belgium in Europe, Israel, Australia and Indonesia, manufacturing a wide range of heavy and household appliances, and usual range of electronics and dipping into mining, and the ever profitable paper making. Oddments were motion picture interests.

By the early 1970s the runaway corporations, more fancifully termed multinational companies, had reached a critical crossroad. The debate in the board rooms was whether to phase out all their domestic state-wide operations and go native in foreign parts. The United States could serve as its tenuous link, its source of more capital and its markets. These decisions were privately arrived at and the population at home had no say in such crucial decisions.

That they were ready to make a fateful (and perhaps fatal) decision against the interests of the United States was indicated in the remarks, annual reports and *inter alia* remarks. The most frequent was that their foreign operations were their salvations. "It pulled us out of the hole." As reported by the *New York Times Service,* "That overseas operations have given a more-than-usual life to the over-all performance of many of the country's multinational corporations has been evident in the recent run of annual and first-quarter earnings report. In many cases the reports have shown gains in foreign business ranging upward from fifteen to twenty-five percent acting as a strong counterbalance of the slacker showing on the domestic side of ledgers. In some industries, foreign business also had offset strike losses." A number of companies reported that their foreign operations were fifty percent of their business and their overseas earnings contributed from seventy-five percent to ninety percent of their profits.

International Business Machines (IBM) showed domestic earnings of $505-million, down from 1969, and foreign earnings of $512.5-million, up from the previous year. Minnesota Mining and Manufacturing and Union Carbide showed heavy gains in foreign business while they were about holding their own in the U. S. An officer of 3Ms International stated: "We are looking ahead to seeing our international business become the greater part of the total than domestic business. We still haven't attained the penetration of foreign markets we want, but I think that by the early 1980s our international sales will have passed the fifty percent mark."

Standard Oil Company (New Jersey) reported that foreign earnings of $681-million were fifty-two percent of the total; earnings of its U. S. operations increased $18-million and $85-million foreign-wise. National Cash Register, an older international outfit, showed earnings of $70-million domestically, down from 1969 and international earning of $73-million, a gain of $15-million. General Electric, the appliances giant, reported that international earnings were up thirty-seven percent, while domestic was up fourteen percent. Dow Chemical Company reported that it expected to achieve the fifty-fifty ratio within several years, as foreign earnings were $115-million while domestic earnings were $144-million.

Entire industries were at the critical point of decision in 1971: to make a last stab at becoming profitable on the domestic scene, or to fold their tents and steal away. The tire and rubber industry centered in Akron, Ohio, put up the litmus paper and a threat in its slogan, "Make Akron Competitive" (Summer 1971). Specifically, the rubber companies wanted their factory hands to dampen demands for more wages and instead deliver more per hour for increased productivity. B. F. Goodrich Company, Goodyear Tire & Rubber Company and Firestone Tire & Rubber Company meant business when they laid off some help, called attention to increasing cost of production, moreso against foreign imports that were rocking the boat. The Akron tire hands were warned by Goodyear that the Watertown, Mass. plant was closed because of high labor costs.

Although imported tires were only 10.6 percent of the domestic market, much lower than the percentage inroad of textiles, shoes, electronics and steel, the tire and rubber manufacturers were realistic enough to know a real threat when it only showed as a speck on the

The Course of an Historical Self-Destruct

horizon. Russell DeYoung, chairman of the Goodyear firm, the industry's leader, warned that "if imports were to keep growing at this rate, they would completely capture the domestic market by 1980." On the other hand, the United Rubber Workers Union blamed the loss of 9,000 jobs to foreign tire imports and faulted, correctly enough, American investments abroad and our giving to favored foreigners (allies) the know-how or more correctly, the technology. Japanese tire imports were outstripping all others and the Akron magnates were openly envious of the $1.75 an hour Nipponese wage as compared to the Akron $7 per hour wage and fringe benefits.

Now that they had a grievance against the alleged low productivity in the old brickwork factories, the high wages and the flood of expected imports, the manufacturers were aching for release from their American prison for the freedom of foreign climes and a yearning eye towards Japan. Nor were the automobile makers reticent or evasive about their urge to cut loose from the restrictive labor bonds in the United States. Henry Ford, II, at his Detroit office May 13, 1971 admitted his pessimism about meeting foreign auto imports. He was concerned with the Japanese imports. "We've only seen the beginning. Wait till these Japanese get a hold of the United States." Foreign cars were running at the rate of a million and a half a year, some fifteen percent of the market. What irked the carmaker was that American small cars, now in proliferation, had not slowed down the small car imports. He blamed rising labor costs for the failure to meet competition on home grounds, warning that manufacturing would lose out totally under such conditions and "we may be a service nation some day."

General Motors and Chrysler Corporation did not send up distress signals, but moved ahead to gain beachheads in Asia and Europe. The former signed for a 34.2 percent interest in Isuzu, a Japanese truck manufacturer and began to explore the field for more acquisitions. The Chrysler Corporation, under heavy financial strain had by August 1971 contracted a financial tie-up with Mitsubishi Heavy Industries, Ltd., buying in for thirty-five percent ownership of Mitsubishi Motors. The Japanese firm had South African and Australian plants, and the Colt and Valiant were scheduled for their assembly lines. Chrysler had also selected the Philippines for an assembly and parts manufacturing operation under the corporate name of Chrysler Philippines Corporation. The outward move was ambitious and Thomas Killefer, Vice-President of Finance, reported August 16, 1971 that Chrysler expected to up its foreign production from one-third of its total to fifty percent within a decade. Ford's tie-up with the Japanese was in proposals to import 160,000 small trucks and buy into a Japanese firm.

The United Automobile Workers, free traders and valiant supporters of free enterprise, were now aroused. They had been tilting at windmills. Now the Rising Sun was in their eyes, blinding them. Primitive in their economic thinking if it could be called that, they were dimly aware, although there were tens of thousands unemployed, that something was wrong. At their international board meeting in Boston August 19, 1971, they called in several economists to unravel the mystery, but they would not abandon their free trade post, which they saw as liberal and which made them responsible men. This despite the warning from a UAW Vice-President of the Chrysler plant, that his men were restive and that the "auto companies are running away and forsaking the American workers." No action was taken.

The Caterpillar Company, makers of road-building and other heavy equipment, headquartered at Peoria, Illinois, made public its annual report for 1970, directed against the equipment division of the Automobile Workers Union. (February, 1971) It was a *cri d'coeur,* albeit a corporate heart. It revealed that the company was coerced in signing a three-year contract for a provision "for unlimited open-end revision of wage rates based on changes in the cost-of-living index." Caught in this bind, which was true enough, Caterpillar sought a way out. As announced in the annual report for 1970, manufacturers competing wholly within the United States have fairly equal freedom to adapt between these two unattractive alternatives. The U. S. manufacturer who exports but does not produce abroad is less fortunate. In competition with manufacturers in overseas markets, he may not be able to raise his prices sufficiently to recover the increase in domestic costs. But those concerns operating on an international scale and having production sources outside the United States do have one other alternative: to do abroad what they cannot do successfully at home.

The argument that there was no alternative except seeking manufacture in low-wage countries was repeated several times. It was evident that the report was a rationale for the moves to foreign ports, already made, as well as the clinching argument for a wholesale or total pull-out from the United States.

It should not be assumed that Caterpillar has been merely waiting for actions by governments or others—at home or abroad—to foster its international business. On the contrary, it has, over the years, established and accomplished a strategic deployment of resources outside the United States. Apart from its strong independent dealer organization, the Company has substantial manufacturing subsidiaries operating in Scotland, England, France, and Belgium, while somewhat smaller units are producing parts, components, or assemblies in Australia, Brazil, Canada, Mexico, and South Africa. Parts warehouses are based in England, Belgium, and Singapore as well as at certain manufacturing plants, while commercial subsidiaries are headquartered in Geneva, Switzerland, and Hong Kong. In Japan, Caterpillar Misubishi operates under the joint ownership of Caterpillar and one of that country's most illustrious business organizations. The results of the operations of that affiliate are not incorporated in the reported consolidated figures, but the venture is now maturing into a successful enterprise from which there can be expected some worthwhile contributions to Caterpillar's future earning power. Another, and much smaller, affiliate operates in India in equity partnership with Larsen & Toubro, Bombay.

Caterpillar officials concluded that they had found their range, and it was outside the States. The more potential long-term significance was the increasing extent to which the controlled overseas subsidiaries of U. S. corporations were becoming capable of producing abroad the equivalent of American-made goods on a cost-price basis which permitted imports into the United States in full and successful competition with the indigenous products. This suggests that the time and the conditions are approaching when greater consideration will have to be given to the selection and use of sources of supply on a least-cost basis—world-wide. What was more, the company felt that it hardly needed the United States for a market, noting that "for the first time in the Company's history, the volume of its sales outside the United States exceeded that within."

With true American ingenuity the pull-out was multi-tiered. The more appealing and immediately profitable course of action was setting up branches or satellite plants outside the United States. It was only an extension of the policy of free-wheeling industries to move from home state to better climes (read states) with fewer taxes and the minimum of harassments (on the pollution problem, etc.). The move to foreign countries was a logical one. Starting with the home continent, there was, of course, Canada, with its resources, as yet unspoiled. Vis-a-vis Mexico, American manufacturers had potted the area south of the border with some 230 branch factories by 1971, small electronics assemblies, finishing off wearing apparel, and toy manufacturers with a total value of $150 million. But it was still less than the value of the off-shore (that is, foreign) production of American manufacturers, valued at $2 billion in 1969.

III. THE WIND-DOWN OF DOMESTIC INDUSTRIES

There are at least a half-dozen paradigms, economic scales or theorems to explain the break-up of the U. S. They all add up to the speed-up of decline and the short shrift given the United States in historical time.

— The wide-bank historical paradigm was that the drive and meaning of American history, its exploitative haste and greed, had run the country into the ground; its vast natural resources had been despoiled, its farmlands had been leached and were in the final stages of fertility.

— The dialectical-Hegelian thesis: At the heart of society was that same demonic rage that cleared and then cleaned out, (leaving as ruins the gargantuan wastes and despoliation of the land and rivers) and was now ready to abandon it for more profitable ventures elsewhere. The historical failure was compounded in the absence of a countervailing force to salvage the country.

— The United States was a contingent and not an historically integrated society. As Professor Sam Bass Warner held of Philadelphia, it was private preserves worked until played out and then abandoned. The successful who garnered the remaining wealth then retired to new climes.

— The classic economic order was fatally subverted for a parasitic, exotic, weapons-systems economy which was self-destructive. This may be subsumed in the Webb paradigm of a closed-frontiers society now bent on consuming itself.

— Professor Arnold Toynbee's famous paradigm reviewed the rise and fall of some twenty odd societies (or nations) that were done in, not necessarily in equal measure, by internal proletariats, disaffected persons, or by foreign (outside) enemies.

As Professor Webb saw it, the closing of the frontiers at the end of the 19th century, thrust the United States into an endemic crisis. World War II catapulted it into the maelstrom of European and international economics, from which it emerged temporarily the victor, an industrial power as opposed to a prostrate Europe. But that was its undoing—the economic system could not be contained within its political and social ethos. The great economic crisis of the 1930s brought the question to the fore even more urgently. Again a world war, World War II, intervened. At its victorious conclusion the question was even more nagging. At this juncture the fateful decision was made, one which had no parallel in history. It was to suborn the normative economic system of commodity production, to a vast changeover to an arms system atomic power, aerospace vehicles and the like. The course of this changeover was traced in *The Fateful Subversion of the American Economy, Consequent on the Gold-Dollar, Trade-Economic and Tax*

Crises (1971). This then would mark the validity of the Webb paradigm of American destiny and provide economists, political scientists and historians with a new paradigm or model.

STEEL: THE UNDERGIRD BUCKLING BADLY

Speaking before the 79th annual meeting of the American Iron and Steel Institute on May 27, 1971, in New York, William J. Stephens, chairman of Jones and Laughlin Steel Corporation, warned that Government policy, if continued, would lead to the self-destruct of the American economy, with steel singled out. He insisted that succeeding Administrations were oblivious to the plight of the industry. He asked for a surcease in taxation of capital outlays, a revision of labor laws to ease the pressure applied by the steel union lobbying for escalation of wages and declaimed against "inflationary wage settlements, specifically those exceeding productivity gains, which cannot be sustained by shrinking profit margins." And then he entered a plea for Government support and subsidy in relocating steelmaking in foreign parts.

Labor, in this instance, the United Steelworkers of America, insisted on their demands for sharp wage increases and the employers, seeing no escape hatch or basis for opposition, gave in. But they insisted on passing the wage hikes on to the consumer by immediate price increases. United Steel reported a drop of profits from 4.5 percent in 1969 to 3 percent in 1970.

A more eloquent and reasoned appeal for help, by

steelmakers still determined to make their stand on native grounds, was by Roger S. Ahlbrandt, president of Allegheny Ludlum Industries, Iric., at a meeting of the World Affairs Council of Pittsburgh May 24, 1971. "There is a pressing imperative for the United States to formulate, as quickly as possible, a strategy and policy for international trade, one which will protect our nation's vital interests, just as the vital interests of competing economies are being protected. The Government must recast its tax policy to encourage the efficient competitor, perhaps through a value-added form of taxation, among others. In addition, investment tax credits and depreciation guidelines must be redesigned to encourage capital investment for U. S. companies to remain competitive internationally. . . .I must say again that our Congress and the Administration will have to look seriously and immediately, at the immediate protection of those of our important industries which have been heavily impacted by imports, in order to stabilize their position while the United States forges a consistent international economic and trade policy."

Pleas notwithstanding, the accumulated impact of the free trade, open-United States-to-our-allies policy, had undermined steel to perhaps an irreversible extent. Following the strike of July 1971, steelmakers realized that they had fewer orders on hand and that the market was weaker than ever because of piled-up stock. Layoffs swept the industry, facilities shut down, furnaces were banked.

Even during the arguments between men and management for new contracts, there was evidence that the industry was winding down from the cumulative effects of importation, disorientation and a growing economic malaise. During July 1971, there were cutbacks for the final closedown of large units. Republic Steel Corporation closed sections of its operation at its Massillon and Canton, Ohio, plants, dropping 3,000 employees and simultaneously laying off 2,000 at its Buffalo plant. Bethlehem Steel, also in the vicinity of Buffalo, closed down units employing 1,000 hands. The Youngstown Sheet and Tube Company closed a blast furnace and three open-hearth units. U. S. Steel laid off 2,000 at its Edgar Thomason works in the Pittsburgh area and another 500 at its Gary, Indiana operation. Earlier, the Wheeling-Pittsburgh Steel Corporation and the Sharon Steel Corporation had announced layoffs.

However, the full impact of the slowdown in the industry did not come until after the new contract with the union was accepted. The steel men realized that it worsened their competitive strength. They could operate only from weakness. The Associated Press reported August 7, 1971: "Six days after the steel industry and union agreed on a new contract without a walkout, tens of thousands of steel workers have been laid off and many hearths are cold, as steel users draw from inventories stockpiled against a strike. Layoffs were not unexpected, but some officials of the United Steelworkers of America said the magnitude of the actions came as a surprise. Others said they saw no reason for undue concern.

"In the Pittsburgh-Western Pennsylvania area alone, an estimated 47,000 steelworkers are either officially laid off or temporarily idled. 'We expected layoffs after the contract but we didn't think it would be anything like this,' said a spokesman at United Steel Workers' headquarters in Pittsburgh. About 34,500 steelworkers in the Chicago area, including the Calumet district of northwestern Indiana, were laid off because of the cutbacks in orders. The United States Steel company announced Wednesday it was recalling only 19,000 of 38,000 employees at two Chicago area plants. It said steelmaking would start again next week but that customer orders would determine the level of production and of employee call-backs."

"Both Inland and Republic Steel have announced layoffs in the Chicago area totaling 15,000 workers, all attributed to a reduction in demand. The bulk of the United States Steel layoffs will be in the Gary plant where 14,000 will be out of work. Mayor Richard Hatcher of Gary said industry sources told him as many as 25,000 persons could be out of work in the city of 175,000 population. As a U.S. Steel spokesman in Pittsburgh put it, there 'simply are no orders and no orders means no work.' The company has an estimated 30,000 workers idle in the Pittsburgh area. Jones and Laughlin, the sixth ranked steel producer, declined to estimate how many of its 10,000 workers in the Pittsburgh area were idle but one source put the figure at about 75 percent. However, the company was in the process of restarting operations and recalling more workers daily.

"Bethlehem Steel's plant in nearby Johnstown remained nearly completely shut down with company officials giving no estimate on reopening. Virtually all of the 6,200 workers there were idle. About 16,000 of 20,000 workers at Bethlehem in Baltimore were off the job with all blast furnaces shut down and all steelmaking furnaces shut down for at least the rest of the week."

TEXTILES: FOREIGN IMPORTS ARE ITS WINDING SHEET

Textiles, the first great industry of the modern industrial age, which in the 19th century made Great Britain the workshop of the world, and in the 20th gave muscle to the growing industrial strength of the United States, had been driven to its last post. In the half century 1890-1940 the South had acquired much of the Northern textile industry, depleting the Philadelphia-Chester area, a premier center for woolens, worsteds and plush weaving, then the great textile centers of New England (Lawrence, Lowell, etc.).

But under the changed economy, textiles were undermined. By 1971 American textiles were in a last-ditch fight against the flood from Asia, Europe and other centers which were initially built up with American money ostensibly to help fight the Communist menace. The $21-billion industry had been drifting while the imported textiles flood was cresting. Burlington Industries, Inc., and J. O. Stevens & Co., the two leaders, showed lower earnings and dividends. The textile leaders expressed bitterness, claiming they had warned of the disaster threatening them, but were not heeded by government officials who had committed the United States to a wide-open market, as the key to its anti-Communist strategy. The textile men, like other industrialists, had indeed been enthusiasts for the earlier schemes, but now they were hurting. Were they to be sacrificed for some dubious allies, in the Grand Strategy to Save the World from Communism? Donald F. McCullough, chairman of Collins and Aikman (plush and other pile fabrics) apparently did not consider it a volte-face. "They (meaning the current and past Administrations) have called us greedy, conniving and downright wrong, but the fact remains that the latest figures (July 1971) on man-made fiber imports are simply staggering. The erosion on our industry is continuing and getting worse." The good allies, anti-Communists all, were sending the greatest amount of synthetic cloths.

The August 15, 1971 emergency declaration by President Nixon only confounded the issue. The good friends, having opened the door, did not want to budge an inch; in fact, they demanded of the hapless colossus that if they were to be kept in line, the despairing creditor (now debtor) could call it. But the locals were getting it in the collective neck. The Southern outposts, the last in the textile industry in the U. S. were being phased out. Burlington closed three plants early in 1971 in Virginia and North Carolina. In the Alabama-Georgia area, the latest to be hit by closing, some fifty mills ceased operations after 1969 and some 27,200 textile hands were turned out, in 1970 alone. These were only the first winds of the coming storm, which would level hundreds of mills like so many ninepins.

CLOTHING: ANOTHER INDUSTRY BEING STITCHED A SHROUD

The men's apparel industry, a $7.7 billion business,

had grown alarmed and restive because of dwindling domestic market and accumulating imports, a precipitate drop from 21.3 million suits in 1960 to 16 million in 1970, and 18 percent down from that figure the first quarter of 1971. A leading manufacturer in the field, Botany Industries, Inc., showed a loss of $3.4 million for a half year ending January 31, 1971. A number of known brand-name men's clothing manufacturers closed shop: Raleigh Clothes, Berwick Clothes and the Timely Clothes unit of BVD. This was viewed as only the beginning of a chain reaction in shutdowns. Style changes deepened the crisis and the eccentric dress habits of the young upset the market. But the imports were hurting domestic sales badly. Men's suits imports were 1.4 million, a fifty percent increase from the 90,000 imports of 1969.

The clothing manufacturers organized in the American Apparel Manufacturers Association, met in Dallas, May 1971, and indicated that they were ready to admit the permanence of imports, and opted for a stake-out on higher price fashion lines. In a review of the domestic clothing-makers plight, the association held that "if nothing is done to moderate the growth of imports in the next ten years, it is conceivable that apparel output and employment could decline by one-quarter to one-third their current levels." The manufacturers, conceding a write-off of much of the domestic product, indicated that they were studying the possibility of establishing plants in European and Asian sewing centers, or importing garments on a larger scale.

ELECTRONICS: YANKEE INGENUITY SHORT-CIRCUITED

The military-industrial complex which suborned commodity production, built an industrial order of the most amazing and ingenious gadgets and devices. The catch was that a vast array of these products had no practical use except for destruction and space travel. In the flush of arrogance of power, the military industrialists proposed to divide the world, with the United States committed to esoteric devices, while the erstwhile defeated and lesser countries were encouraged to make the little things sold in the marketplace. It was at this point that the Yankee ingenuity which had created a machine civilization was ground down into the mud. It was true that the larger electronics corporations kept going in the strength of their small utility commodities, but, because their big money came from M.-I. contracts and the ownership of the broadcasting industry, the commodities could be ditched when they paid less and less. The later phase-out of large segments of the electronics industry, because of high-capital costs, was inevitable.

The electronics industry in the commodity-use field felt the onrush of Japanese, other Asiatic and European competition which during the 1960s pushed the domestic product to the side and flooded the American market. The Electronic Industries Association, the trade organization, reported that in 1970 imports were thirty-four percent of the market for TV sets, thirty-one percent of TV picture tubes, forty-nine percent of resistors, sixty-four percent of capacitors and ninety percent of transformers.

The Course of an Historical Self-Destruct 51

During October, 1970 *Samson Trends,* a technological trade journal, reported that consumer electronics imports was a $1 billion business and that the domestic manufacturers were throwing in the towel. Besides television sets and radios, the foreign importers were contesting the audio equipment field. Imports accounted for sixty-three percent of phonographs, ninety-two percent of radios. The future was not in doubt any longer as *Samson Trends* announced: "Consumer electronics is a dying domestic industry." The surviving industries moved on to foreign parts and labeled items, manufactured in Taiwan and in Mexico, "Made in U. S. A." On the domestic front, the shut-down of electronics plants were like falling dominoes. General Electric closed its integrated-circuit plant at Syracuse, N. Y., October 1971, and in January 1972 shut its Buffalo transistor plant. Earlier in 1970 GTE Sylvania, Inc., phased out its semi-conductor plant in New England and its Batavia, N. Y. plant, and RCA shut down its solid-state component part plant in Cincinnati.

IV. SERVICES AND GOVERNMENTAL OUTSTRIP THE PRODUCTIVE – LIVING BY TAKING IN EACH OTHER'S WASH

The American industrial order matured too quickly. Its decadence was marked by the overwhelming rise and spread of the service businesses. A society in which the more vigorous, the middle classes, take in each other's wash, was too maturated for continuance or growth. Then, too, the services were not ancillary to commodities production, but were excrescences of it, products of the vast excesses of government, of a gargantuan war production and military organization, and as a result were parasitic on the fundamental commodities economy.

Dr. William C. Freund, economist of the New York Stock Exchange, commented on the crisis of the municipal service unions insisting on ever higher rates, "How can we meet the problem of inflation stemming from the services industries? Ours is a rapidly growing service economy, with increasing proportions of national income being spent on health, transportation recreation, education, police protection and the like. It is precisely these services whose costs are skyrocketing. The costs of services has shot up 113 per cent in the last two decades, compared with forty-seven per cent for commodities and thirty per cent for durable goods."

Freund would have services costs closer to the commodities line, and he would have it by a greater productivity in non-commodity areas. The rub was that services, for those mostly in higher income brackets, demanded an increased correlation, often above the manufacturing sector. "The problem in the service industry, especially in the provision of governmental services, is the difficulty of matching the productivity gains achieved in manufacturing." The comparison was not true—it would indicate that the economists did not know of the qualitative difference, and to suggest that services be subject to the man-hour production, was being ignorant of the nature of non-commodity services.

The basic manufacturing centers were winding down. In Pittsburgh, where more wealth had been generated in the basic steel and ancillary industries than perhaps any other location in the country, the industry in 1970 was living off its past achievements. The steel and allied industries were phasing out and there was little hope of an increment of jobs in industry. Employment of whatever notice was to be had in the services. By 1970 there were 590,000 employed in non-manufacturing, the production jobs having fallen from 343,000 in 1957 to 275,000 in 1970, making it sixty-three percent in services and thirty-seven percent in manufacturing, whereas in 1950 it was evenly divided.

In New Jersey there was a startling reversal within the 60's decade as reported by Ronald Heymann, Labor and Industrial Commissioner. He indicated that whereas it was formerly 60-40 in favor of manufacture, the services had preempted the lead at 60 percent. He blamed the depletion of manufacturing to foreign imports, including footwear, textiles, electronics and chemicals. In New York, the wind-down was in a cutback in defense contracts, the leveling down of steel in the Buffalo area, and the depletion and pull-out of the clothing industry in New York City. Louis L. Levine, New York State Industrial Commissioner noted that the "defense bubble could burst again" urging diversification. In Connecticut the wind-down was even more drastic and the unemployment figures higher, about twenty-five percent in some localities.

Andrew Stein, State Assemblyman (D.) from Manhattan warned in mid-1971 that New York State was rapidly devolving in economic viability. The shrinking economic base was overwhelmed by excrescent growth of government and service employees, swamping its productive cover. "New York State actually experienced a decline in the number of manufacturing jobs, from 1,878,000 in 1960 to 1,769,000 in 1970. . . . While economic activity in the private sector had turned sluggish, government expenses have moved steadily upward. In 1960, total expenditures of state government were $1,902,600,000. By 1970, the figure had climbed to $6,274,800,000." The result was a dismaying charade. The erstwhile Empire State was "now increasingly dominated by the helplessly poor, by civil servants and retirees."

A study by Constance Sorrentino, an economist with the Bureau of Labor Statistics, contended that by 1970 sixty-two percent of the labor force in the United States were in the service employments. She held it was characteristic of the developed countries. "Only France, Italy, Japan and Germany continue to have more workers employed in the production of goods than of services. Japan and France appear likely to become service economies during the 1970s. But Italy and Germany will probably not shift until later, because service employment constitutes only thirty-eight per cent of total employment in Italy and forty-one per cent in Germany." Miss Sorrentino categorized the services as those of transportation, communication, public utilities, trade, finance, public administration (i.e., government) private household services and miscellaneous. In her comparative study Miss Sorrentino like the economists, made the same basic error in classifying the military/complex industry and employment, as productive.

The parasitism of the services (termed white collar) was evident in its growth in relation to the decline and phase-out of the productive jobs. The white seeped through the narrowing area of the blue and threatened to gray the remaining industrial scene. This was true of the older industrial sections of the country. In a piece from a study by the Pennsylvania State Employment Service, Peter H. Binzen, staff writer for the (Philadelphia) *Evening Bulletin* came up with some deductions illustrative of the sweep of the white collar menace (February 23, 1972).

"In the last twenty years, the size of the work force in the eight-county Philadelphia labor market area has grown by twenty-five percent. However, employment in service industries ranging from nursing to catering and private security work has risen by ninety-five percent. State and local governments, including school districts, have grown by 131 percent, or more than five times the overall expansion. One result is that those with local, state or Federal Government jobs (269,600 persons in 1971) now outnumber workers making nondurable goods (252,400 persons). And the combined total of public school teachers, others with government jobs and those in service industries exceeds the manufacturing work force by more than 20,000 employees. There are now 591,800 working in government and service industries compared with 573,600 in manufacturing. Yet twenty years ago there were almost 240,000 more manufacturing jobs in this area than jobs in government and the service industries." The labor market included five counties, including Philadelphia, and three counties in New Jersey adjacent to Philadelphia.

The cancerous growth of the government-service businesses initiated by the American scheme of choking its productive forces and spreading to Western Europe, was too marked to be gainsaid. *The Times Literary Supplement* for June 2, 1972, described it as "The Runaway Leviathan." It was regarded as an international phenomenon—"there will soon be no more 'free,' representative, private-sector-cum-parliamentary society on our side of the Iron Curtain." Dealing with recent studies of British and Western economies, the reviewer indicated the deadly deadweight of the new economy. "The private sector still turns out six-sevenths of the national income or output, but half of its output (three out of six-sevenths of the national income) is taken by public authorities and redistributed 'non-productively' in the sense that no new measurable wealth is thereby created; and most of the one in four who work for the state and its purely governmental administrative or redistributive agencies are thus employed. No other leading Western nation, not even socialist Sweden, places such a burden upon its productive private sector; for even in Sweden less of the national income is turned out or handled by the public sector."

In the United States the matter was rationalized and declared the mark of a higher technological society. Dr. J. E. Goldman, senior vice president for research and development of the Xerox Corporation, speaking at the Philadelphia meeting of the American Association for the Advancement of Science (1971) admitted that "the production of services exceeds the production of physical goods: the values of services are now a larger component of our gross national product than the values originating from manufactured goods. All indications point to further dominance by the service sector. This remarkable evolution has important implications for technology. It tells me that the impact of technology on the economy in the next decades will not come primarily from technology's function of enhancing manufacturing productivity. Rather, I believe technology will be directed toward the improvement of services, or, more broadly expressed, improving the quality of life."

Whatever hope and comfort scientists and government people sought to gain from a topsy-turvy economy dominated by the services, it caused havoc on the mundane political level. The First National Bank of Boston, in assessing the situation in its New England

The Course of an Historical Self-Destruct

Report for August 1972, found the Massachusetts state fiscal budget for 1973 two and a half times the size of the 1967 budget. Unemployment was up 100,---, local property taxes second highest in the nation, and welfare costs on a runaway course. Describing this as a destructive cycle the report traced its downward course. "Our economy weakens as state government spending grows out of control. As the state takes over an ever-larger portion, the private sector is crushed under the burden of supporting extensive government activities. Then some businesses move to more favorable economic climates in other states, and the support burden on remaining business is increased. One statistic summarizes the situation: State tax payments per person employed in the private sector of the Massachusetts economy have nearly doubled since 1967. Clearly, the brakes must be applied to the juggernaut of state spending while the spending machinery and appetites for new programs are reexamined."

V. OBSOLESCENT U.S.A. – OR INDUSTRIAL MIGHT UNDERMINED BY THE RIGHTEOUS

In the two decades from 1947 (the date of the Truman Doctrine) when American commodity production was being driven out, diverted to a sidestream in favor of military, aerospace, atomic and other non-commodity production, there was no protest or even warning of the consequences. But when the frantic changeover had worked its way and was suspected of leading to economic disaster, here and there a hue and cry went up. There was the grudging admission that commodities were the stuff of trade, money and life. The alarums grew apace when it was realized to what extent commodity production had been undermined, ruined, phased out. It was a startling realization when it was noted that Germany and Japan, the two defeated nations, allowed no armaments, were now the leading commodity producers—but the correlation between war-systems industries and commodities industries was not granted, or admitted. The professors of economics side-stepped the subject by ignoring it; to do them justice one would have to point out that they could not discuss a matter which they did not understand.

With so many leading industries phasing out extensive

units and divisions because of competitive imports, and fleeing the country to set up business in cheap-wage climes, it was a wonder that there remained a residual industrial plant. The viable plants were working at 65-75 percent of capacity and feared that within a decade half of the industrial capital would be dead capital. The surviving industries and their many ancillary and auxiliary industries saw their fate tied up with greater productivity per man per hour. Their sights were set on the German-Japanese industrial axis. Labor had to be threatened, cajoled and enticed to come along on this survival program but many industrialists despaired that labor would buckle under and shoulder the burden.

The intellects of the industrial order, as intellects go in a pragmatic environment, i.e., McGraw-Hill Publications Company, industrial, trade and book publishers, alarmed the industrial community of the need to gird their loins for the true Armageddon. In a newspaper advertisement October 12, 1971, McGraw-Hill insisted "American industry is losing the lead. It must be encouraged to step up plant improvement, if it is to stay competitive and boost the real income of labor." The American way of life was in danger, McGraw-Hill averred, "our prosperous American way of life is in jeopardy because our efficiency is no longer what it should be." There was real trouble ahead. "Much of our plant and equipment is simply too old. From 1960 to 1969, the U. S. devoted only 13 percent of its Gross National Product to private investment in those facilities which modern business requires. In the same period, Japan was putting 27 percent of its output into such investment, West Germany 20 percent, France

18 percent." The U. S. trailed last in efficiency, increased productivity or output per man hour. "Far from stepping up investment to meet the threat of overseas competition, U. S. industry actually will be putting less new equipment in place this year than last. In manufacturing, where the competition is toughest, the reduction in new plants and equipment is greatest." The Administration's move for accelerated depreciation and an investment tax credit was held to be of immediate help in refurbishing antiquated plants.

McGraw-Hill ostensibly back-tracked on its earlier figures of planned capital investment. In a report by Douglas Greenwald, chief economist of the company "the planned increase for 1972 is significantly higher than what was estimated last fall." Important sectors, however, planned a decrease, including the non-ferrous metals industries, iron and steel and electrical machinery manufacturers. The increase occurred more often in the non-manufacturing industries.

In sharper delineation, the maturation and obsolescence of the older sections of the country was indicated and often emphasized, moreso by the investing community. Richard D. Hill, chairman of the First National Bank of Boston held in late 1971 that "the current economic transition problem in New England is unique among all states and regions, because our regional economy has moved into the final phase of the development process; economic maturity in a mature economy. The central issue is the maintenance of growth." What the banker meant was that older industries, textiles and shoes, were winding down, the military-industrial contracts following. In consequence, one million people, "one-fourth of our labor force" were currently underemployed while the total number of unemployed was one-quarter million. Hill saw possibilities in new industries, lumber and wood products, printing and publishing, metal products and machinery. The Middle Atlantic States, too, may be taken as in "the final phase of the development process," losing industry to the South and West.

DEAD CAPITAL MEET DEAD LABOR: THE PHASING OUT OF AN INDUSTRIAL ORDER

The changeover of the economy, hidden under apocalyptic cover was never acknowledged and the delusion persisted that it was the traditional economy. In consequence, economic reports, studies and policies were erratic, self-delusory and often obfuscated. Groping in this self-induced miasma there was no objective view; the economists, businessmen and accountants subserving, such a view, could not even with the best intentions face the elements of simple reality. The Penn Central railroad bankruptcy was a case in point. Under the rubric of a juncture of two giant railroads with a capital of $7 billion, the nominal parties involved could not, even when faced with the evidence, see through the precipitate decline of the rail system due to the vast subsidizing of the aircraft industry, the costliest of the military/industrial complex. Business and economic reality, though given even more symbolic and algebraic sophistication only muddled any insight into the economic breakdown. Again in the instance of the Penn Central there was only the Sunday afternoon announcement of the board of directors that the greatest line had no means to continue. There followed scandals of stock manipulation and the pullout of insiders but withal no one in authority would admit that for all its book capitalization, it was not live capital. There was no study, no analyses by economists, busy tracing the causes of the collapse. The receivers stumbled on a truth, that its labor force was for the most a dead force not conforming to its economic needs. But the brotherhoods, remnants of what was termed the aristocracy of labor, in their turn, refused to face up to it. Instead they consolidated their position and struck or threatened to strike, for wage increases up to thirty percent. The laborites who were the baleful force which pushed to the utmost for the economic changeover that undercut all, did not want to play the game now that phase-out was in the books. But then dead capital could not move with this albatross around its neck. The 1970-71 stock market losses of some $375 billion indicated the extent of dead capital nationwide and its overweight crashing through all supports given it.

RAILROADS: SCRAPING THE ROADS OF DESTINY

The railroads opened up and tied together the continental expanse, sited its major villages and towns and hurried industrialization. It was the linch-pin of a surge of industrial development and was acknowledged as such; its executives, king-makers in the heavy industry states; its labor, the aristocracy who would have little to do with the lesser breeds. But with the undercutting of the traditional economic order, the economic basis of the railroads was also cut to ribbons. No one, least of all the economists, recognized its grievous decline as the result of the sustained undermining of its unique function by government-supported aviation and highway construction large-scale trucking. The face of God was turned away from the instrument of classic modern civilization.

Like all else on the economic scene, no one, least of all the railroad nabobs and the economists at large would face up to the crisis. Yet it had to confront them eventually. When it did, as in the case of the Penn-Central debacle with its revelation of inside financial jobbery, it was accepted passively and fatalistically. There were no post-mortems, but a patchwork reorganization of sorts with an interim quasi-government organization termed Amtrak to maintain the fiction of railroad passenger travel. John Burby, an assistant to Alan S. Boyd, first Secretary of the Department of Transportation, tried to put it in perspective in his study *The Great American Motion Sickness: Or Why You Can't Get There From Here* (1971), in which he described the railroad system—a $500 billion investment—as "An indifferent, inefficient, dirty, smelly, expensive, noisy and often destructive and deadly beast of national burden that goes where the spirit of speculation moves it or where it is driven by vested interest." Burby called for a planned transportation policy with the allocation of transit systems arguing that it would be responsive to the private capital market system. But he failed to indicate the extent to which the market had abandoned railroading in this new economic system spawned by the military-industrial complex.

There was no lack of last-ditch troopers in the ranks of railroaders and their financial compeers. One such, Arthur D. Lewis, a former president of Eastern Airlines, asked and proposed to answer the question: "How can a service so vital to national health and well being be so sick financially and unproductive for its investors?" He was in favor of planning, via a regulatory system, a quasi-public private corporation, a mixed bag as it were, which hurried him to disclaim its implications. "Some would say that this is nationalization with all its horrors. But this would not be true. INTRO (his proposed Integrated National Transportation Resources Organization) would conform to the present trend, in which government provides a general concept of direction and a general funding capability while private enterprise takes the responsibility for satisfying standards of service and developing earnings to stimulate investment." That is, to reclaim the castout and restore it to its rightful place in a more orderly society. But that was the catch, Lewis would have order suspended in the chaos of the present.

Perhaps Robert A. Nelson, former director of the Office of High Speed Ground Transportation, saw through the destructive contradictions. The railroads, still the only reliable transport for bulk commodities, "have been able to survive the sharp increases of real wages since World War II by using up their very large and extensive physical plant, downgrading their traffic consist and obtaining very substantial increases in output per employee through technological advance. All three of these methods may have just about run their course. The plant is very much worn down; it is difficult to visualize new sources of traffic, and no technological changes are in sight comparable in impact with that of diesels. There are only a few places in the United States where the total disappearance of rail passenger service would cause more than minor inconvenience." More crucial was the role of freight transit. To be viable, that is profitable, it required constant replacement and new road facilities. The old could not be seen even as earning their upkeep. Nelson then quoted the Interstate Commerce Commission in 1963, which "estimated that reproduction of depreciated road and structure at that time would cost more than $33 billion, compared to its book value of $14.1 billion." Capital support investment for such replacement would hardly be possible in the market because of uncertainty that even with a refurbished plant the railroads could prove profitable. Public support by government taxmonies at the Federal and State level alone could fund the refurbishment. Nationalization, or para-socialization, would only find support from those industrial sectors in need of mass freight carriers for their industries. But whether they could carry weight in government circles committed to the automobile, highway construction, air transport and travel, was the crux of the problem.

THE NEW CABAL: AUTOMOBILES, OIL AND THE HIGHWAY BEHEMOTH

As Lewis, aforementioned, put it, "the automobile absorbs 89 per cent of all passenger transportation expenditures and hampers the achievement of balanced transportation services based on the best contribution that each can provide." More than undercutting the railroads, the automobile and truck had thrown their counterweight against rail surface travel; they became the principal indicator of economic viability, and with the highway building consortium and the oil companies profiting, the automotive business became the very heart of the new economic order. The trucking industry proposed to take over larger segments of heavy over-the-road hauling, pushing for ever larger trailer trucks, and in Oregon triple-trailer trucks were authorized. Encouraging them was the commitment of 80 percent of all Federal monies (excise taxes on gasoline, oil, vehicle use, truck weight and on tires) to surface transportation by the National System of Interstate and Defense Highways System. Some 45,000 miles of superhighways were proposed under the act of 1956 (Highway Trust Fund) and expected to be completed by 1975 at a cost of $43 billion.

The automakers during the 1960s and into the 70s were laying the ground for a massive move out of the United States. Their outpost foreign manufacturers whetted their appetite for more; the pressures on them here to introduce a pollution-free automobile, a $65 billion charge as Mobil Oil Company asserted, and the high-wage level of unionized labor was a tightening noose. Henry Ford 2nd, chairman of the Ford Motor Company, which had the widest spread of foreign subsidiaries, was articulate in the growing dissatisfaction with the American scene. He defended at every turn the foreign ventures, holding it was for the good of all in the still-valid American commitment around the world. He equated automobile prosperity with the national good. In a year-end 1972 statement the Ford Motor Company struck out against the profit-margin ceiling set by the Administration. "It must be eliminated or substantially modified next year if business is to make it. It can eliminate the incentive for additional efficiency improvement in those firms that have been most successful in improving their efficiency." But there was no letup in harassments. Ford was penalized $7 million in February 1973 with an assortment of criminal and civil fines for violations of the Clean Air Act, the charges being tampering with autos to be tested. A week later the company warned it "has been backed to the cliff edge of desperation" and demanded a relaxation of regulations set for 1975 to forestall "a complete shutdown of the United States auto industry."

THE STRUCTURALLY UNEMPLOYED: NEW ESTATE OF THE WELFARE STATE

There was no greater horror in modern industrial society than to look upon the multi-faced Head of Medusa, that is, the unemployed. There were attempts to distort the image through quick-change mirrors. The efforts to meet it and to hide it were frantic and frenetic as well. It underlay the vast economic changes indicated in the creation of endless parasitic governmental and service industries. But with the limits of the changeover to the military-industrial economy and its accompanying non-production, and, with the breakdown of the productive economy, it was now structurally visible and statistically definable. Even so, efforts were made to hide these facts by resorting to self-deception and to the deceitful, confused assurances, oft-repeated, of the economists. The very volume of such efforts in the 1970s was numbing. Even the reporters who lived through and by such news gagged at its wild inconsistency. As Edwin L. Dale, Jr., *New York Times* economic reporter wrote: "The nation, certainly the Congress, is being swamped with figures and analyses of the unemployment problem. They are enough to numb the mind. The Congressional Joint Economic Committee so far this month alone (February 1971) has had analyses from four Cabinet-level officers of the Government, a member of the Federal Reserve Board and seven private economists."

At least one official believed that it was a cover-up, but then he was concerned with the pressing crisis of mounting welfare relief. Jule M. Sugarman, Human Resources Administrator of New York City, estimated January 13, 1972, that there were 500,000 unemployed, 250,000 more than the officially recorded. This was a discrete item, the million and a quarter on the official welfare roles, primarily of the dependent kind, consisting mostly of a million-plus Negro women and their children. Sugarman then urged directors of Federally-financed jobs across the United States to halt the migration to New York which was making it the most gigantic almshouse in history. He further contested the official figure of 5,000,000 unemployed and added 1.5 million "employable welfare recipients," more than a half million youth between sixteen and nineteen who were not at school and 750,000 single adults and married women who quit seeking jobs. (The New York Department of Social Services reported 1,251,482 on the city's relief rolls January 1, 1971, budgeted at $1.9 billion of whom 876,199 "were in the aid-to-dependent-children category.")

The fear of unemployment was politically deeper and more pronounced since the redundancy was not that of a depression or more severely a crisis, but that of a washout of industries as such—structurally, that is, signifying permanent unemployment. In point of fact Operation Cold War in switching the economy, was to stave off the windup of industrial U. S. A. The redundancy of the changeover was absorbed by the vast incretion of the service and/or governmental jobs, to the point where they became seventy-five percent of the working force. At this fateful juncture the remaining industries were in a vicious squeeze and the only future was that of wind-downs and closures. The resultant unemployment then, is that the unassimilated help was so much detritus.

THE PATRIOTS DEPART THESE SHORES IN SELF-RIGHTEOUS HYPOCRISY

The $85 billion American foreign industry had gotten on so famously, or more correctly infamously, that by 1972 it was selling $68 billion products as against the $27 billion exported from the domestic scene. At this rate it would cut down U. S. exports to the trickle of a minor country. Taken with the flood of imports of foreign owned and manufactured industries, it would be the final, perhaps, fatal twist of the vise around American industry. The Administration truckled to the self-righteous and echoed their arguments that foreign imports made it imperative for survival, that American industry get a new competitive superiority in foreign parts. The betrayal was glossed over, and painted as salvation.

The Commerce Department, in a staff study made public January 30, 1972, urged the arguments for the mass displacement of American industry, to still the anger of organized labor finally convinced of their sell-out by their fellow conspirators in the anti-Communist crusade. "Those import categories which have experienced most rapid growth and are perhaps most responsible for dislocations of United States workers (for example, textiles, shoes, steel and automobiles) are overwhelmingly the output of foreign-owned enterprises, not of United States-owned affiliates." The report placed the American foreign corporations in the role of saviour to the remaining American industries in that their American based plants had a higher than average viability and employment. "To remain competitive at home and abroad in products for which wages are an important component of total costs, United States companies often have no alternative to transferring to lower-wage foreign areas. If the products in question were not produced and supplied from abroad by United States affiliates, they would likely be supplied by foreign competitors. The choice, therefore, is often not between United States or foreign operations, but between foreign operations and no operations at all."

No death sentence had ever been spoken in so bland and toneless a manner. Had all the heroics gone out of a people facing the worldly apocalypse?

The wider and more intensive the move-out from the United States, the more the corporate giants and their auxiliaries felt that they could justify it in the name of the common good. The resort to such sophistry was dumbly accepted, but the facts were too stubborn to be denied for long. Much emotional fervor for their cause was evinced at the National Foreign Trade Council January 3, 1972. The Council's key stand was to hit back at proposals to limit the flow of American investments abroad. One official declared that "these investments have a long-range favorable impact on our exports, jobs and prosperity at home. Their expansion is essential to preserve its worldwide competitive position." Then, in a statement, the Council warned: "Protectionist proposals for further restrictions on United States investments should be rejected as harmful to our own economic stability and growth and to America's role in the growth of the world economy."

At a White House Conference on the Industrial World Ahead held in Washington, February 8, 1971, attended by some 1,500 businessmen and labor leaders, Carl A. Gerstacker, chairman of the Dow Chemical Company, saw the major industries of the future as anational, or without any nationality. "My first and most urgent recommendation to this White House conference is that we establish a basis upon which we can make truly neutral, truly anational corporations a possibility, and not only a possibility but a reality. The anational company may be the major hope in the world today, for economic cooperation among people, for prosperity among the nations, for peace in our world. I have long dreamed of buying an island owned by no nation, and of establishing the world headquarters of the Dow Company on the truly neutral ground of such an island, beholden to no nation or society."

Even after the realignment or devaluation of the dollar by ten percent, the multinational corporations were eager to continue expanding their beachheads and inland junctures in Europe, Asia and other foreign parts. Their officials in Europe had indicated that they preferred the looser controls over business and manufacturing overseas, and were not harassed by the rising emphasis on consumerism or better products and the enormity of anti-pollution costs. What really warmed the cockles of their hearts was that Europeans and other non-Americans really worked at their jobs and strove for increased productivity, also, union pressure was not so unreasoning and labor costs were considerably much lower. One official, quoted in Paris (December 27, 1971) not eager for his anti-American bias to show through, put their euphoria diplomatically, "We still see basic structural problems in the United States economy which will take a long time to straighten out. Europe will probably be faced with similar problems at a later date. But, as of now, we still see no better place to invest."

If the post-Smoot-Hawley protectionists and believers in America first still believed that home industry was the American faith and fate, they were to be cruelly disillusioned when the United States Chamber of Commerce lined up with the up-and-outers who would shake the dust of a has-been country. Again it was delivered by a survey, now the favorite intellectual component of the business world, this time made by the Chamber. Arch N. Booth, executive vice-president of the C of C was triumphant. "This survey refutes the charges being made by the A.F.L.-C.I.O. that U. S. multinational firms are exporting U. S. jobs, reducing exports and flooding the U. S. with imports."

All of this would indicate that industry and business, even those with troubled consciences, were irrevocably committed to clearing out for greener pastures. If the leaders of American society were dead-set on a clear-out what was to stop the disintegration of that society? Purportedly there were a handful of old timers, representing the fears of the older, smaller family-dominated manufacturers and businesses, and tagging along, organized labor, the wild-eyed hardhats who had led the march for free trade in the Truman-Kennedy-Johnson days. They now knew they were betrayed. Their boss-buddies had gone on to bigger things leaving them with closed factories and mills and a future of pacing long lines of welfare relief.

What fight there was, was centered in the Foreign Trade and Investment Act of 1972 introduced by Senator Vance Hartke, senior senator from Indiana, and Representative John Burke of Massachusetts. In a piece explaining his reasons (February 27, 1971), Senator Hartke held that "during the decade of the 1960s, more than a half million jobs were lost to imports, many in industries where parent firms invested abroad and then imported to supply the domestic market. This type of behavior is encouraged by present tax laws and trade policies. More shocking yet is the fact that modern technology, often developed with the substantial participation of United States tax dollars, is licensed abroad at the expense of domestic employment." Hartke realized that our tax laws were making overseas investment more attractive. Another point in contention was that while "most countries regulate their technology and carefully control outflows of capital, America has largely left these matters in private hands. Plants are closed, new inventions are immediately licensed overseas, workers are thrown out of work, and all because of some private calculation of short-term profit. There is no reason that the world's greatest democracy should leave her trade and investment policy in the hands of a few." The Hartke Act would vest control of the flow of capital and technology in the President, and restrict imports.

Gaylord A. Freeman, Jr., chairman of the First National Bank of Chicago, would put up the industries of the country for purchase in stock blocs to Europeans and others holding dollars. He scotched the notion that the vast pile-up of paper dollars was worthless because incontrovertible. Referring to the going industries, (mentioning General Motors) he made the point "this is America's real asset in the world." He would sop up the ever growing pile of deficit dollars in a swap arrangement. As put by a finance reporter "he would have the United States Treasury buy up packages of corporate securities and offer them at a discount to foreign central banks." But then the Continental banks had been doing that on a limited basis—investing in securities, buying U. S. Treasury bills and bonds—but hardly enough to level down the mountainous rubble of dollars. The European central bankers would be more receptive as the deficit totals continued—a case of a half or rather a three-quarters loaf being better than none. The Japanese, too, were alert to the possibility and their bankers were suggesting loans to companies willing to buy (the polite term was invest) into United States industry and business. The prospect was terrifying— given the present level of deficits and opening up the purchase of American industry stock and bonds with the money, the foreigners would hold a hundred billion dollars equity within five years. And then the deluge!

Freeman made the proposal at a meeting of some fifty American businessmen with their European counterparts in Versailles, France, March 2, 1972. This meeting could properly (that is, historically) be termed a plot, brazenly and openly arrived at, to dump the U. S. and use it for a dumping ground. Any hint of opposition to this design, such as the Burke-Hartke Bill, weak and indeterminate (coming from the double-crossing, self-crossing labor forces, historically more reactionary than our able two-timing bankers) drove *les Americains* to a frenzy. The latter spent much time telling their faithful new allies they would down the Hartke forces, the rest of their time plotting their course of integration into the European market.

At this juncture it would be helpful to indicate that the top corporate businesses, industries, and the leading banks were in the front phalanx of the internationalists. The opposition to the sellout from the industrial and business elements was primarily from the ranks of the left-behind sectors, hardly given to standing up to their corporate betters. Some opposition came from the business journals and the McGraw-Hill outfit. The internationalists had the sweep of the prestigious daily newspapers with *The New York Times* in the lead. Editorially the *Times* savaged the standup laborites and the Burke-Hartke Bill declaring that "the bill, if passed, would be a disaster to the American economy, to labor and the consumer alike." It was compared to the Smoot-Hawley Act of 1930, which "worsened the unemployment problem" then.

CLOSING IN ON THE PREMIER SECONDARY DOMESTIC FIRMS

The growth of the military-industrial complex supported the steel and the heavy machine industries. But, counterproductively, as the cant had it, it undermined the ancillary industries that were the sum and substance of the older commodity order. The tens of thousands of supplier and subsidiary sub-contracting firms that were the backbone of the middle order of industrialization were now dependent on the m/i system. They entered the m/i orbit where there was not the traditional competitiveness and order of utility and cost accounting of the commodity market. Those machine firms in the commodity market suffered by proximity and/or emulation of the m/i productive order.

The Singer Company, the 125-year-old sewing machine firm, that had a monopoly in its field as chief supplier of the sewing industries and domestic use, was also a household word the world over. With the turnabout of the American economy it diversified into the new-fangled office machine business while its premier rank as manufacturer of sewing machines was undermined by Japanese, Italian and German imports. By 1970 it was a conglomerate with $2 billion in annual sales, but with its sewing machine and consumer products in difficulty. Sears, Roebuck & Company, importing Japanese sewing machines, now had 25 percent of the domestic market, the German and Italian imports taking another 33 percent, leaving Singer with 42 percent of the home market. For the moment Singer held its edge in exports but the same factors that pushed it out of the domestic market could be expected to squeeze its hold on the foreign market. Its Friden business machines division was lost in the proliferation of the computer-calculator-business machine firms, where it was among the lesser breed.

The great retail establishments were caught in the crossfire of the built-in-inflation of the military-industrial order, the disarray of commodities production and the growing dependence on foreign imports, and the retail practices and markups of the older order. Internally there was the rise of the discount practices— slicing the traditional 100 percent markup to 40-50 percent — made possible by newcomers who did not have a built-up hierarchy of services and bureaucracy. Sears, Roebuck & Company and the Woolworth Company, more than held their own because of their long tradition of foreign imports and marketing, and minimum service surcharges, originating specifications for manufacturers (making the latter beholden as suppliers) that could meet the discounters. But the big city department stores did not have these advantages. Their charges and overhead were geared to a middle-class clientele. When the latter departed the cities for the suburbs, the department stores followed and evolved chains strung along the suburban shopping centers. The discounters followed them and pressed them competitively for the middle business. Gimbel Brothers, which went public, was hard hit by their attempt to meet the new competition, losing out on their extended credit system which accrued a loss of $6 million in the 1960s. Its stock was selling at less than the book value by 1972.

The $72 billion food business was similarly caught between inflationary price costs and compensatory reorganization to cut down the surcharges of the older economy. The process was damaging. The Great Atlantic & Pacific Tea Company, the largest chain, had heavy going and reported a quarterly deficit of more than $20 million for the first quarter 1972. This was in the face of record sales, but the cost of changing over to new, leaner stores termed WEO (Where Economy Originates), were necessarily high. Food stores were assured of sales but the squeeze between costs and competitive prices loomed as their dominant problem, going into the 1970s.

The passing of the old order received little attention but in the middle ranks of Middle America business, manufacture and commerce there was a sense of defeat, muted, disoriented, nostalgic for the orderly past. The military-industrial order had laid waste to Middle

America but there was no fight in the middling classes. They were done in not from without, but from within, not having an historical sensitivity to see it as a betrayal. In a piece in the *Wall Street Journal,* August 8, 1972, "Modern Times in Cedar Rapids," Cyril L. Kegler, chairman of the board of Bishop Buffets Inc., of Cedar Rapids, Iowa, ate his heart out, but blamed no one but impersonal forces. Referring to the death of the city's "last remaining important industrialist" Howard Hall, Kegler wrote that it symbolized the passing of the old order. "I refer to the period when all our communities over the country contained a wide range of small to medium manufacturing enterprises" making for a progressive social order. "Then the change. One after another, these successful manufacturing enterprises fell into the hands of the big-monied conglomerates."

The Hall enterprises, Iowa Manufacturing Company (Amana refrigerators) and Iowa Iron and Steel Works became Raytheon subsidiaries (the electronics company nurtured by military contracts). The "big financial swingers" as Kegler termed them, also cut a wide swath through the "important and successful restaurants" and retail establishments; then, in the retail business, including that of appliances, automotive services, etc. Give the country's big department store chains—Sears, Wards, Penney's, etc.—a continuation of their expansion of the past ten years, and they will have pretty well scooped in all the business that used to be done by the thousands of small local retailers. . . .Everywhere we look we see evidence of the accelerating shift in this country from business run by people—lots of people—to those owned and run by a very few business giants."

IV. ALL MONIED HANDS PREPARE TO ABANDON SHIP

Bankers had played an uncharacteristic role in turning viciously and irresponsibly on the verities of the traditional economic order of which they were presumably the keepers. They made a mockery of gold, calling it a base metal, while flooding Europe with paper currency based on gold by international agreement. They aided and abetted the desperate irresponsibility and culpability of three Administrations in trampling on traditional banking practices, agreements and international conduct. Such brigandage piled up vast dollar deficits burdening and undermining the monetary stability of the Western world. These depredations, carried out by blackmailing the receiver nations, finally ended in the unilateral declaration of the default and bankruptcy of the Bretton Woods agreement. If bankers indeed had a leading role in the American economy, they failed at it to the puzzlement and bewilderment of Continental bankers. They were no more than rube bankers, village financiers at once lost and destructive on the international scene.

In the present interregnum of monetary chaos the bankers and others with money to burn took a dim view of the domestic economy in their jurisdictions and opted for a move to new El Dorados. They were not social ameliorists or philanthropists, nor willing to be tied down as nationalists of their own country. By the closing years of the 1960s they were ready to abandon ship and to console the abandoned natives, invited European and other moneyed nations to invest in the United States for a try at working over the remaining pockets of profitability.

They began with the New England area, which had been worked over, lost its premier textile position to the South and its boot and shoe business to foreign imports. It was a bleak prospect for the bankers, but they were not daunted. The First National Bank of Boston, the largest in the Northeast and its holding company, First National Boston Corporation, had $4.7 billion in assets and $4 billion in trust funds and were "facing a serious earnings squeeze" (August 27, 1971). Cautiously, so as not to alarm the timorous, the bank declared its earnings basis "outside the slow-growing area" and proposed to go in for national factoring (buying up accounts receivable from profitable areas) in the United States. The Boston bankers indicated that in common with others they were looking to foreign investments. First Boston intended to expand its mutual-funds business in Brazil and invest here and in Argentina. Eastward looking, they had tied up with factoring and finance companies in some thirty foreign countries.

The big New York banks had long held the internationalist view and they were in their element in pushing the frontier of investment from out of the United States, to the Continent. The Chase Manhattan Bank, the premier Rockefeller bank, had long been in Venezuela and in other oil countries. (The dominant Rockefeller interests were always oil) Morgan Guaranty, the successor Morgan company—the self-styled corporate bank—declared that foreign grounds were home grounds. Making a pitch for businesses bent on making the foreign scene Morgan warned there were complex problems needing experienced judgment. "Morgan Guaranty, with years of experience in international banking, is uniquely qualified to help you make these judgments (on foreign investments and businesses). In fact, we've been in international banking since the eighteen-sixties when J. Pierpont Morgan started in New York with close ties in London and Paris." Not mentioned was that the flow of money was the other way—from Europe to the United States in investments and loans. Again Morgan came up with the same figures—they had their fingers in the pie in some thirty-one countries. Other New York banks were not abashed in announcing that they were going to the places and climes where the action was. Manufacturer Hanover declared itself doing "big things internationally." In Philadelphia the largest banks, Philadelphia National and Girard Bank (formerly Girard Trust Company) were garnering their resources to join the Eastward hegira.

Having worked up a rationale for a mixed bag of internationalism, and hopeful of profits outside the United States, the bankers were not adverse to a *quid pro quo*. Why not let the Europeans, the oil-rich Arab nabobs and the Asiatic magnates, get a piece of the action of what was left for profitable picking in the U. S.? They showed good fellowship and welcomed foreign bankers and industrialists to have the run of the States if they could spot opportunities. Not that the Continentals *etal* had not already established beachheads (true the Germans and Japanese received rebuffs when they planned large complexes but only because of a new awareness of the need to protect the ecology and water supply). It was a binding *quid pro quo* in following two decades of huge deficits when the Treasury urged key dollar holders to buy up U. S. obligations and through the backdoor get into American industry (or what remained of it). Those Europeans who used their own and U. S. gift-money for a market play lost their shirttails in the Long Drop of the stock market 1969-1970, but they had more dollars on hand. The overall picture was that the accumulated and current capital had been depleted some 10 trillion dollars; and furthermore, the makers-and-shakers became determined to use the remaining and new capital in profitable ventures overseas. There was a capital vacuum—moreso because of the second and third time around exploitation of remaining resources.

The money capitals of the Continent were alert enough for the occasion. Brussels, sprouting with news of the growth of the ECC, moved in on the scene. As early as 1968 four European banks formed a consortium, boasting a capital of $16 billion, moved in on Wall Street, opened an American office and cautiously, for a starter, committed $70 million. The managers of the beachhead were duly diffident. "We are not here to compete with American banks. The idea is to give Europeans who want to set up affiliates in the United States the kind of help they cannot get from banking head offices in Europe." Another service would be to help American investors move on to the European scene. The banks were the Midland Bank of Great

The Course of an Historical Self-Destruct

Britain, the Deutsche Bank (of Germany), the Societe Generale de Banque (of France), and the Amsterdam-Rotterdam Bank (of the Netherlands).

The move took hold and more foreign bankers moved in on Wall Street. By September 1971 there were two newcomers, the French Credit Lyonnais which announced the opening of a branch office and its German partner, Commerzbank, caroled that it "ist jetzt ein New Yorker." The first German bank (from Hamburg) offered "a complete range of banking services" working both ways across the Atlantic. Then the two were joined by the Banco di Roma (of Italy) for a "tripod of cooperation." With this initial setup who could deny the ECC bankers, the world or the United States? But these were not the only goodies for the thrifty burghers. They were encouraged to move in closer, as when the New York Stock Exchange approved the bid of a Belgian firm to buy into a leading NYSE firm. The Compagne Lambert pour l' Industrie & la Finance, through its American branch acquired a minority interest, but it was a foot in the door. The Japanese, now the greatest industrialists, were urged to move in on the fabricating sector. Mitsubishi Aircraft International staked out a factory in San Angelo, Texas, for turboprop executive planes.

By the Summer of '72 the banking pack was in full swing. With 600 units in operation in foreign parts—and more planned—the bankers were in heady euphoria. What a contrast to the domestic scene! Here at home the leading bankers were fretting at the narrowing fields of investment and the piddling and dwindling rate of growth. Earnings were in large measure derived from ever heavier portfolios of U. S. obligations and mortgages—a dead end business. Basic capitalization loans—the real meat of the banking business—now depended primarily on endless renewal of the schemes, plans and operations of the military-industrial complex, a pigs' fight to get to the public money trough.

Overseas there was genuine banking and high swinging profits. As Edward P. Foldessy, staff reporter of the *Wall Street Journal* (May 26, 1972) put it "banks have been all but falling over each other in a rush to open branches and acquire subsidiaries abroad. Foreign earnings of the seven largest U. S. banking concerns rocketed an average of 30 percent from a year earlier. Moreover, the gain came at a time when domestic profits were registering a two percent drop." Foreign profits were an increasing share of total earnings. Bank of America: 25 percent in 1971 from 20 percent in 1970; First National City Bank of New York: 42 percent from 38 percent in 1970; Chase Manhattan, 20 percent from 15 percent; J. P. Morgan, 30 percent from 25 percent; Manufacturers Hanover, 28 percent from 24 percent; Chemical Bank (New York), 15 percent from 10 percent and Bankers Trust, 23 percent from 16 percent.

The fly in the ointment was the precariousness of the dollar and the growing importance and weight of European currency. There was the possibility that if it continued, the American bankers dealing in dollars for the most part, would be undercut or bypassed. But in mid 1972 the bankers were flushed with new conquests, and touched wood in their panelled offices, hoping their luck would not run out.

VII. THE ECONOMISTS AS YES-SAYERS AND DUTIFUL POLLYANNAS – AND FOOLS TO BOOT

Caught in the trap of the makings of two previous Administrations, the current one could not help but blunder in the growing maze. For moral support they had their economists. Government and official economists were, as all officials were, hapless apologists for their betters. But few officials had such a bewildering set of circumstances to explain away. What they fobbed off were not historical *explanas,* but good cheer and reassurances which the populace wanted to hear. The official Nixon view, stated in late 1969, was "that the economy will be good in 1971, and we will have a strong upturn in 1972." The selective support for this projection was evident during 1970 and 1971. The schemata was simple: find favorable indicators and gauge the GNP (Gross National Product). The academic economists followed suit, but with the admixture of obscure mumbo-jumbo, and economic trivia. And in the wings there were honors and prizes for the economists emeriti. Professor Paul Samuelson of M.I.T., a mathematician, received a Nobel Prize. Professor Simon Kuznets, retired Harvard economist, who won the Alfred Nobel Memorial Prize in Economic Science (1971), for his "empirically founded interpretation of economic growth which has led to new and deepened insight into the economic and social structure and process of development."

Therein hangs a tale. The Swedish academicians and the American economists were so taken with GNP at this juncture because it was the linchpin on which the American economic theories rose or fell. The paradigm was distilled from Dr. Kuznets' *National Income and Its Composition, 1919 to 1930* (1941) which lumped production and services in a common pot. The GNP schematic served to cover and obscure the divisive changeover in the economy to military-industrial production. Thus the parasitic and the productive lumped together, never gave a clue to the destruction of the older commodity production. In short it was an almost foolproof device for not differentiating and detecting such differentiation. It was the principal device in the slight-of-hand trickery to hold off doubts, because at every turn the Writ was trotted out and sure enough the GNP was up or inching up no matter what the situation abroad, with industries ruined and sold out. The trick was that the loss of productive industry led to a multiplication of service and government jobs, which were one and the same with the GNP thermometer.

Before hearing from the independent economists and writers, it would be instructive to listen to Eliot Janeway's view. Janeway, an independent economist, had occasion to measure the official financiers and economists in the Johnson Administration, as falsifiers and deceivers in their obscuring of the President's secretive siphoning off billions under false pretenses for the

Vietnam. In short his economist *entourage* covered up what in other more sophisticated times and more mature nations would be high treason.

"America's present moral and political crisis is the direct result of President Johnson's conspiratorial decision to manipulate war under cover of peace and, worse still, to escale it by stealth and to finance it by budgetary embezzlement....Against this background of Presidential arrogance, the ranking member of the quadriad—the Secretary of the Treasury, the chairman of the Federal Reserve Board, the chairman of the Council of Economic Advisors and the director of the Bureau of the Budget—made a sorry record for irresponsibility and incompetence....Pride goeth before a fall. The card-carrying members of the econometric model-tenders' union have enjoyed the pride, and they are suffering the fall. Costly though the coming shakeout in the stock market and the economy will be, the deflation in the mystique of the econometric model-tenders is fated to be even more so."

However the econometrics of the Nixon Administration had a shame-faced role, as well. To spread cheer when there was no basis for it, was to pabulum-feed news of evidential crisis. Their opposite numbers in the private businessmen's organizations fell into step, keeping up the pretense that recovery was around the corner, in the face of ever-mounting bad news on the economic front. For instance, the 1971 meeting of the Conference Board, a brainier business study group, asserted good prospects for 1972: an increase in the GNP to $100 billion, prices held down to three percent increase from 4.5, and the leveling off of unemployment from six percent to five percent.

The academic economists were forever trotting out new testimony to the effect that all was well. Trotted out, for at no time had the economists been held as oracles—but now the official circles turned to them to allay fears and put their imprimatur on statements, reports and interviews that glowed with Rotarian optimism.

The academic economists formed a solid phalanx in support of official economic views, sniping at each other over the usual esoterica of the trade, but pronouncing a benediction on the economy. There was new interest in the late John Maynard Keynes who as editor of the (British) *Economic Journal* spread the gospel of public spending to take up the slack of the economy. At the Bretton Woods conference he had proposed a new international money system and a universal money unit termed bancor. For the most part, the professors took the now enshrined GNP as their crucial criterion and since it was always up, although not at the rate they hoped for, they always had good news in the background. Others propagated the earlier notion of the world divided into spheres of specialty manufacture, with the U.S. shorn of the homely commodities and devoting itself to the exotic war-related products.

Thus they never saw or even glimpsed that an historic fissure marked the economy, that the old was fatefully compromised. Hence, they blundered along in their GNP wonderland refusing to see the manifest realities of growing bankruptcy and depletion of the nation's basic industries and its irresponsibilities leading to the break-up of the international monetary order. One maverick, John Kenneth Galbraith, a Harvard economist, did glimpse, although not full-faced, the head of Medusa, and urged public spending for public needs and nationalization of the m/i industries (which would integrate it even more as the dominant economic force).

The bank economists were another phalanx in support of official trumpery. *Citibank,* economic review of the First National Bank of New York (November 1971) gave financial editors a rousing lead and a field day for head writers—"The U. S. economy looks like a winner in 1972." The bankers saw "real output in 1972" with inflation and unemployment held down. They also issued a stern warning that "the greatest danger is a resurgence of inflation in late 1972 and in 1973 when the margin of slack in the economy has been significantly reduced." Other leading bank reviews followed the now rutted line.

My favorite bank economist, Frederick Heldring, vice-president of the Philadelphia National Bank, who during 1971 spoke and wrote on the economic crisis, was more historically analytic and critical. In a newspaper piece in the *Evening Bulletin* (Philadelphia) during October 1971, he reviewed briefly the monetary crisis of the 1930s. "In the 1930s one international monetary system died. Before another emerged, a world recession developed. Now that we have suffered a breakdown of the system that followed, will we repeat the mistakes of the 30s? It must not happen again. . . .The outlines of a new system are beginning to emerge. The dollar will not play the central role, but will be like any currency. . . . In retrospect, the biggest error we made was to render Marshall aid to Europe as gifts. . . .We received no mandate to fight a war in Vietnam."

When the stock market sank to the 800 mark in mid-November 1971, the economists sprang forth with their explanations. Again the First National Bank economist manned the breach. "The stock market pessimism is perplexing. It is running contrary to all the optimistic forecasts on the economy. I think the economy will do very well next year and it is running pretty well now." The economist for the du Ponts was full of cheer. He saw the GNP rising and inflation down. The reason for the pessimism was "that people are looking backward at the long sequence of difficulties our nation has been through in recent years." The implications were that the worse was over, the Wilderness traversed and the Promised Land in view. An extraordinary interpretation of the crystal ball.

And then, to the secret despair of the knowing economists at Columbia, their old colleague, Arthur Burns, chairman of the Federal Reserve Board, pontificated, as a para-governmental official, that the economic scene was heartening. There were "many reasons for being optimistic about the future. As economic recovery accelerates, we can be fully confident that all classes of income, including corporate profits will rise. This outcome depends, however, on our achieving success in the struggle with inflation....The financial climate is conducive to economic expansion."

The economy may have been buffeted by destructive forces but up on the bridge the professional economists saw a calming sea. Their reassurance was an amazing performance. Apparently they could not see what was evident to the grubbiest of financial reporters, that from every quarter, inside and out, the economy was riddled, bedeviled, scuttled and wrecked. Thus the twenty-fifth annual meeting of the Economic Forum of the Conference Board, January 3, 1972, (another elite businessmen's sonic boom sound board) found the professors, bankers and corporate top hats forecasting that, the GNP, would climb another $100 billion in 1972. When the bankers-professors-businessmen triune went for cutting analysis, the play-limits were sharply demarcated. It was autos, new home starts, money supply. Thus Solomon Fabricant, professor of economics, New York University declared: "There has been all kinds of hesitations in the recovery because of special factors, some of which have been mentioned, but there is a momentum built in through the cumulative rise in the money supply, order for new homes, a very low inventory level which will provide some push as we look ahead and accumulate shortages of all kinds." But then Louis J. Paradiso, economic consultant, did not see any momentum, neither in consumer spending and new orders for capital equipment. "This has been very erratic. What else? There has been a momentum in housing all through this year. But, apart from that, where is the momentum? Professor Fabricant would emphasize the importance of housing starts and its effect on "manufacturing and other industries!"

The real questions were only posed, some indicated doubts of all optimistic forecasts, but then they were not explored. It was a banker, Walter E. Hoadley, executive vice-president and chief economist of the Bank of America, who sent out a series of questions, but it was evident that neither he nor his fellow bank economists were ready to follow through. "Hasn't the position of the United States in the world deteriorated sharply and permanently deteriorated? Hasn't the freedom to manage and really to improve productivity been seriously reduced?"

Seeking a consensus of corporate elite and economists to solve the mystery of the economy, *Time*, not to be outflanked by boozier compatriots, saw "1972 will be the year of real recovery. That's the unanimous opinion of *Time's* Board of Economists (the first group to announce, early in October, the now-standard forecast of a $100 billion G.N.P. rise) and of most other analysts as well.... The outlook for the economy can be summed up simply: growth. New Government stimulation of the economy is one main reason. The tax cuts (for business write-offs) which have just been signed into law, special programs planned to create jobs for Vietnam veterans, the international currency agreement." The *Time* crystal-ball gazers saw "profits before taxes leap by between fourteen and seventeen percent, capital spending by business will jump by between nine and eleven percent. Auto sales should almost equal, perhaps exceed last year's 10.2 million. Housing starts, which hit a record 2.2 million in 1971, will slip, but housing completions will rise to 2.1 million. Exports should surge ahead of imports again by anywhere from $1.5 billion to $3 billion, creating more sales for domestic companies and more jobs for workers." (January 3, 1972)

The academic economists, and, tagging behind, the political economists have moved to the forefront as government advisers since the days of the first great crisis, the crash of the 1930s. The Council of Economic Advisers has been an important backstop since then and even moreso in the 1960s; but the more remote, theoretical brethren in their ivy towers worried about the outcome. Two pieces in Spring 1972 called attention to this queasiness and fear of the underpinning of the discipline (and by extension the intellectual enterprise of the universities). Professor Joseph J. Spengler of Duke University put it as hubris (unwarranted arrogance) which classically came before a fall. "The Great Depression of the 1930s, together with the resulting increase in public employment, augmented the demand for economists, and their number increased. They could not acquire much influence and administrative leverage, however, until macroeconomics of Keynesian and post-Keynesian vintage had come into being and general acceptance and governments had assumed a great deal of responsibility, particularly for maintaining so-called full employment. Only then could hubris begin to flourish among economists. Neither Walras nor Marshall fathered hubris. It was Keynes who made possible the rise of an economic mandarinate, together with an intellectual climate conducive to hubris and its capacity for generating negative as well as favorable externalities."

The government had become the arbiter and referee of economics, with employment at all costs and under all circumstances the goal. The Employment Act of 1946 was "to promote maximum employment, production and purchasing power." Spengler saw through the military-industrial complex, though he does not use the term, contending that "Even as war and governmental whim create an unstable economy often too dependent upon highly specialized and inflexible industries (such as the aerospace industry) that tend to collapse upon withdrawal of support, so does inflation generate an unstable economy prone to shrink upon withdrawal of its unnatural and necessarily transitory stimulus." But things went awry, the economists not knowing the answer. "Confidence in federal management of the national economic framework, whipped up by the New Frontiersmen and their fellow travelers in the early 1960s, has since been dissipated." A good word need be said for Professor Spengler—at least he was groping for the answer. Most were too cock-sure about their GNP models. He is for "guarding society against the evil effects of hubris" and called for "corrective action," if only to save the virtue of the economists, whom he lumped with the social scientists, "since the recurrence of the adverse effects of unwise policies imputed to social scientists could destroy confidence in their skill and thus deprive society of what it badly needs." The admission was surprising—no fraternity brother had faulted the economists in summary fashion. It was more than a credibility gap, it was a paradigmic and discipline gap. By extension it could pull down the intellectual scheme that was the university.

"There is need for at least three courses of action." But it was not addressed to the basic assumptions of the GNP economics, rather it was political. "Decentralization of economic and political authority and decision-making would be most effective." It was a case of turning back the clock or breaking it. "A reversal of the centralizing trends underway for nearly three centuries

The Course of an Historical Self-Destruct 99

thus is indicated, together with the cybernetizing of vast, insensitive, and ever-expanding federal bureaucratic structures (such as the Department of Defense) and the diminution of the national managerial and fiscal role of the state, currently lauded by social scientists as well as by subjective proletarians and lumpenintelligensia." The economists, if they were to be true to their *raison* should have traced the course of the breakdown of the traditional order to the new exigent order that was historical disintegration. The State was the power and the force that enforced the changeover, a case of historical self-destruct in the Hegelian sense.

The put down of the economists by Peter Wiles of the London School of Economics reflected that, at the academic high command, there was a loss of faith in and disillusion with, the discipline (including political economy). Granting that its methodology was advanced and that economics is "no longer the jackal at the feast of mathematics and statistics, but the lion himself, hunting new prey and providing the feast,"—there was still a narrowness and self-preoccupation that foreclosed the discipline. The error or lacunae that was to be its undoing was that while "economists try to deduce complicated and yet practical conclusions, useful in real life, from much ratiocination and few data," there was still a crucial gap. "Our energy goes into the ratiocination and we do not examine the data. Nay worse, we confine our questions to those that can be answered in this manner." A circular paradigmn was self-defeating.

Academic economics as a cover for the policies of the devolution of the traditional American economy, was rife with dissenters who sensed something fundamentally awry. Mancur Olson and Christopher K. Clague in their study "Dissent in Economics: The Convergence of Extremes" held that "great as the prestige of economics is in comparison with the other social sciences, most economists readily concede that there are many inadequate models, dubious assumptions, and areas of ignorance in the discipline." The authors singled out the dissenters, to the right and left of the prestigious center. The left was given form by the Union for Radical Political Economists founded in September 1968. They were aligned with the center in demanding more social welfare and their economics, a soft neo-Marxism, saw the economy as the old classical one. As such they were even more purblind than the regulars. The right was what they conceived to be the traditional free market, less governmental intervention and less warfare monies diverted from their laissez-faire use. The divergence was political—none questioned the assessment of the economic facts.

And then why didn't anyone interested in the fate of economics and the state of the Union remind his fellows about the advice and warnings of the late Irving A. Olds, chairman of the board of the United States Steel Corporation 1940-1952? Olds in 1952 in a piece, "Inflation or Free Enterprise" held that "inflation is invariably government-produced. It originates with the profligate expenditure of government funds and it always follows war, because war, of course, is the most wasteful expenditure of a nation's resources—financial, material and human." From then on, the spiral to destruction is inevitable. "Confiscatory and ruinous taxes" are levied on its "most productive citizens." "Inflation and taxa-

The Course of an Historical Self-Destruct 101

tion, together, quickly despoil the accumulated savings of the people, and destroy all further incentive to save, to invest, or even to produce. Without new capital there is no way to buy new tools of production, except out of profits; and profits, of course, have been largely eaten—or taxed—away." Then Olds had it in for the government and academic economists. "So at this point the patient is clearly *in extremis.* The government sends for its High Priests of Economic Mumbo-Jumbo and instructs them to find a cure. Now I do not know what devilish perversity of human nature is responsible for this fact, but nevertheless it *is* a fact that, for about 4,000 years, these Economic Witch Doctors have invariably come up with the same prescription." And that is wage controls and price freezes.

Olds was perhaps the first industrialist to see the government as destructive of industry, but he did not grasp the historical forces which had forced the governing element to turn on its ground. "Anything which increases the federal deficit is inflationary, and is, therefore, undesirable. And anything which discourages private investment will curb production, and is, therefore ruinous. . .I am going to draw heavily upon experience—the experience with which I am most familiar—the experience of United States Steel; but remember, if you please, that what is happening to our business is also happening—or may well happen—to every other business in America." Olds revealed that U. S. Steel had spent more than a million capital for production and planned three-quarter billion more for this purpose. "For every dollar we paid in dividends to our common stockholders last year (1951), we paid five dollars in taxes to the Federal government. But that is only the *first* tax on our earnings. One of our shareholders—who is in the top income brackets where new capital should be most readily available—wrote me the other day saying that out of every dollar *he* received from us in dividends, he had to pay ninety cents to the federal government in taxes. So, in the end, he got ten cents out of the $6.00 we earned before taxes, and the federal government took the other $5.90—or fifty-nine times as he retained. The chance of expanding our productive facilities out of profits is becoming even bleaker. In the first place, much of our so-called profit now has to be used merely to replace the existing tools of production as they wear out."

Despite their persistence in sticking by their models, paradigms, scales and thickets of figures, the economists glimpsed Limbo. No one dare mention it and never referred to what had happened to the generation of economists who were swept into the dustbin with the economic crisis of the 1930s. The public, of course, had no memories, its economics lying closer to the survival level whose greatest moment of economic truth was to pick a winner at the track. Occasionally there were pauses when economists realized they were standing within the shadow of the gibbet. The late Professor Frank Knight, doyen of the orthodox school at the University of Chicago, compared his fellows to augurs of ancient Rome (rogues and fools) in his Presidential address to the American Economic Association in 1950: "I have been increasingly moved to wonder whether my job is a job or a racket."

More recently Professor Robert A. Solo, professor of

Economics and Management at Michigan State University essayed "The Collapse of Establishment Economics" (1972). He began with a wholesale write-off of established economics. "It comes down to this: the Establishment economics that is taught in the universities, proliferated in the journals, regurgitated in the councils of government, with all its mountains of published outputs, has not advanced our capacity to control the economy beyond what it was in the late 1930s. That after the clear failure of the neo-classical and Keynesian concepts and techniques of monetary and fiscal control, the nation is left with no answer to the persistent and profound economic problems of inflation and unemployment save a wage-price freeze in the manner of World War I or World War II attests to sterility of economic thought and policy. So does antitrustism, cast in the mold of the 1890s and allowing no role for industrial policy except to preserve market competition. In fact, the attack on monopoly has foundered of its own ineptitude, although the ritual threats continue. And when faced with a truly dangerous phenomenon, such as the conglomerate mergers of the 1960s, produced by financial manipulators making grist for their security mills, the professional antitrust economists were silent. Like other realities of a modern enterprise, this phenomenon, which will probably subvert management effectiveness and organizational rationale for generations, is outside their conceptual framework."

Establishment economics failed in getting at and implementing policies affecting the gold standard, deficit financing, monetary controls and the like. "The real complexities of real economics elude us. . . .Why have economists been unable to look at new problems with fresh eyes? What has kept conceptualization and assumption invulnerable to the evidence of experience or the commonplace observation of day to day?" Solo saw it as the elaboration of purported laws and scales to repair the debacle of the 1930s. He singled out Professor Paul Samuelson of M.I.T. who, he held, recast economics "in complex and esoteric mathematical symbolism" which was circular and led up a blind alley. "The energies of generations were consumed not in a search for truth but in displays of virtuosity. Who can wonder then that 30 years of intense activities by Establishment economics has produced little of substantive significance."

VIII. INFLATION BUILT IN BY THE PARASITISM OF THE M-I COMPLEX AND THE OBSOLESCENCE OF COMMODITY PRODUCTION

It was during President Johnson's Administration that inflation was given official recognition as the cause of the economic distress. Growing numbers of his critics did not hesitate to call him the wildest inflator of all. The economists, on the other hand, had only the old elementary explanation that it was the squeeze of too much money backed by too little goods. This was elaborated on but only made a more confusing and hopeless tangle. The classic *explanas* could not explain the unclassic background of today's inflation. Edwin L. Dale, Jr. *The New York Times* reporter who wrote endless reams on the money crisis, serving only to further muddle the subject, admitted that "an enormous amount of intellectual energy has been devoted to the question within individual countries—it is a nearly universal problem—and in international bodies. No sure answers have emerged." The Marshall school of economics, with Keynes thrown in, could not explain it. "Why did a severe slowdown in the economy, with painful unemployment, not at least produce a payoff in the form of much-reduced inflation?" The answers were in the daily news and such mini-studies that were ventured in the daily press and journals of opinion. With $300 billion a year, spent on armament and ancillary waste for two decades by the two blind giants (U. S. and U. S. S. R.) and the rest of the world spending proportionate sums, the cause of inflation was no mystery.

Inflation was, of necessity, the principal ingredient of the changeover of the economic order from commodity to arms production. The vast and overpowering monies for the latter were a heavy charge against the ever narrowing band of commodity production. As the new order with its military-industrial base grew in wide concentric circles, the inflation in turn became built-in, progressive and cumulative. The two-decade changeover, resulting in nearly seventy-five percent of the wage earners becoming engaged in military and esoteric industries, the burgeoning of the services and governmental services industries, and the fourteen million on welfare or outside of any gainful employment, was too ponderous a weight for commodity production to carry. There was never in any society, such an excessive number of non-producers relying on the devolving and deteriorating commodities base. And all this was legitimized and bureaucratized by government sanction in the use of tax monies, nearly one half of the total Gross National Product.

So the tortuous floundering about continued—for no one in responsibility was willing or ready to admit its historic cause—while the economists as medicine men of the tribe poured the soothing syrup down our throats. Occasionally there was an admission that the whole thing eluded them. *Time* magazine lined up a list of economists to discuss "Inflation's Stubborn Resistance" (December 14, 1970) "unexplainable by the philosophy of Adam Smith, John Maynard Keynes or even Milton Friedman, a new strain of inflation has become a reality for millions of Americans. So far, it has proved stubbornly resistant to the classic remedy of business slowdown that has cured inflation in the past."

The wage-inflation pressure mounted steadily with the non-producers becoming better organized, articulate and a political power to be reckoned with. Before President Nixon proclaimed his emergency New Economic Policy, the rate of money being poured into the economy was running at nearly fourteen percent when it was admitted by the Federal Reserve that only a six percent increase was safe. The President's unilateral decision (the Congress has alas been phased out of meaningful politics) was at last an admission that the economy was in critical condition and all salvage efforts were aimed at holding inflationary pressure down by pacing wages and prices.

The bankers who had aided and abetted such perfidy and wickedness by flooding Europe with $100 billion paper dollars now declared inconvertible against the pitiful hoard of $10 billion in gold, were in on the salvage act, known in Wall Street parlance as Phase Two. That was the interim when wages and prices were to come under control. Sidney Homer, a Salomon Brothers (Baltimore bankers) limited partner admitted that there was no point in going on to later phases until wages and prices were under manageable control. "The traditional economic causes of inflation do not exist," Mr. Homer said with less than Homeric wisdom. "There are few or no shortages, demand is flat, there are no surpluses of things and surpluses of labor." This would again indicate that the bankers, along with the economists, did not know what had happened to the economy. A case of blind leading the purblind. Mr. Homer saw it as a psychological reaction. "Our authorities must first realize that they are dealing primarily with a psychological problem of expectations. Their words and their deeds should be expertly planned with this in mind. They must aim to create a climate where future inflation is not universally expected."

LO THE DYING STOCK MARKET – THE DRYING UP OF PUBLIC CAPITAL

The near-collapse of the stock market with a loss of some $375 billion in an eighteen-month period, the receivership of the Penn Central Railroad and the mounting number of other large corporations in economic stringency and short of capital, occurred during the summer of 1970 without much comment and with stunned acceptance. The explanation offered by government economists was that there was a liquidity crisis caused by inflation, which explained nothing. It was basically a dehydration: the drying up or the admission of the ineffectiveness of the older capital structure underlying the undermined, by-passed industries, the deadwood created by the New Economic Order. It begat a chain reaction and some economists, peering cautiously ahead, held that at least one-third of the leading corporations were veering toward insolvency. Kenneth B. Smilen and Kenneth Safian, investment advisors, put it more slickly. "Our economy started in the early 1950s from an historically high level of liquidity, which had been built up during the depression and the war, and progressively exhausted these resources during the 1950s and 1960s. Finally, in an attempt to continue the momentum of growth, an impressively heavy layer of debt was placed on top of the full utilization of capital."

The liquidation of the older economic order by a New Economic Order based on the military-industrial complex had no point of definition, for it was effected by an economic cannibalism and abandonment of the older industries. The effect on the New York Stock Exchange, the principal exchange, was disastrous and far-reaching. The collapse and liquidation of leading Exchange firms followed, with some 17,000 employees of member firms losing their jobs and another 15,000 people in auxiliary or businesses serving NYSE firms thrown out of employment. Some 173 member firms were wiped out from 1968 through 1970.

With such liquidation the some 31 million investors were badly hurt and became distrustful of the market. Paradoxically there was little or no panic and apparently the losses were accepted with stoic patience. Nonetheless, there was an underlying fear that did not surface too readily (the economists were atypically quiescent). There was doubt and fear that the public issuance of capital had been compromised and that the traditional economic order was in jeopardy. There was a veering toward bond or debt financing for capital accretion. Corporate liquidity was then the problem facing surviving industries, except the m/i industries which fed on tax monies.

The stock market business was in distress and during

the 1970s and 1971s there were a series of reorganizations; the stabilization of remaining firms and discussions to take measures to repair the damage and to eliminate the practices of a bull market. It was now a political issue and the Securities and Exchange Commission entered the scene following on the report by William McChesney Martin for reorganization of the ground rules, with a recommendation to exclude financial institutions from exchange membership. If anything, it indicated the changed nature of the buying public. This was best analyzed by Thomas J. Holt, a determined self-taught young man who proved his perspicacity by organizing his own advisory service. In an interview during September 1971, Holt, now dramatized as Wall Street's super-bear said, "It's not a matter of whether a broad-scale collapse will take place, but when it will start and how deep the plunge will be." His advisory service recommended short sales. "The whole trouble with the market is that it's entirely illiquid at this point. I mean not very much buying power is left, but a whole lot of stock is overhanging the market." Individual investors had been quitting at the rate of $10 billion a year and the market was kept alive by a conglomerate group of institutional investors, mutual funds, insurance companies and private pension funds. The institutionals kept the market going, mutual funds being subject to a heavy drain by redemptions. Insurance company purchases averaged $2 billion a year, as did pension fund buying. "But now public liquidation has increased and at the same time the institutions have little buying power left and some may

The Course of an Historical Self-Destruct

even turn to net liquidations, especially if mutual-fund net redemptions should pick up."

Holt did not mention one other source of support for the stock market: purchases by foreign investors, although they dropped from a high of more than $2 billion in 1968 to a half billion in 1970. Behind this loomed the possibility of foreign stock buying, moving in with a broad-band movement of a foreign take-over of given sectors of American industry. The Europeans and other creditors still had a wad of $100 billion by 1973 American dollars for free spending, if not redemption in gold.

Behind the residual capital market supported by the big four financial elements aforementioned, there was the rapid growth of a new market. The SEC officials termed it a hot issues market that had gotten underway in the late 1960s, "the sonics and the tronics of the 1961-1962 and 1967-1968 markets." The surviving corporations and the viable military-industrial conglomerates searching for new capital were issuing stock like mad generating a volatile but active market and helped it recover when it went below 800. The SEC threatened to keep an eye on the new companies issuing such stock. As William J. Casey, chairman of the SEC put it, it was for the protection of investors. He insisted that the new ventures show their qualifications and responsibility. "And if, indeed, there has been no market research, no budgeting, no evaluation of technology, the investor is at least entitled to know that. I believe this inquiry and its conclusions can be important in focusing investment funds and corporate responsibilities on worthwhile objectives—and avoiding future investor losses on the scale experienced in the last few years."

It was a losing game all around, although none of the participants would admit it to themselves, much less to the public. The Blue Chip corporations had been chipped of their sheen and more importantly of their earnings and hid shamefacedly from themselves and the public. They were intent on phasing out domestically and going abroad. They were not of the stoic breed to go down with a sinking ship. The military-industrial complex, the new economy that had been the root of all this evil, were a tarnished lot: militarily inept and a savage fraud, industrially piling up vast stores of armaments, but doggedly demanding their annual tribute of $100 billion plus, their stocks had lost their glamor in the debacle of 1968-1969.

The Götterdämmerung of American capital, some ten trillion, was the most astounding case of self-destruct in history. What was there left for continuation and survival? The people's savings? For the most that was in insurance and savings accounts. The former had ventured into the stock market and got burned in the turn-down of 1969-70 and in 1971-72 became one of the mainstays of the market. The savings accounts were mostly in government securities and real estate mortgages but that was not primary capital. Generated profits? Under the Nixon-fixed economy plan that was to be circumscribed. New capital growth was winding down, limiting still further the scope of surviving industries.

Two generations ago cities and states skirted the constitutional limitation on tax rates by creating quasi-

The Course of an Historical Self-Destruct

public authorities and commissions with authority to raise moneys and exact fees. The larger cities survived, after a fashion, by this parallel system of tax exaction. The Federal government likewise created a parallel system, outside of the nominal and official budget. While Federal credit raising, dispersing programs and bureaucracies originated in the New Deal, it was in the beginning only a fractional part of the budget. By the time of the Nixon Administration, however, it was a parallel system that overshadowed the constitutional budget, itself the major force in the money market at a $250 billion deficit. By the early 1970s the more vigilant bankers were alarmed at the spread of the extra-budgetary credit programs.

Dr. Maurice Mann, executive vice-president of a Pittsburgh bank, speaking at a symposium sponsored by the Federal Home Loan Bank in Washington during August 1972, revealed the extent of the bankers' fears. "In recent years there has been an explosion in the number and dollar size of federal credit programs. In addition to serious economic and Federal budget consequences, this development has contributed to the burgeoning of Federal government and Federal-supported credit demands in the nation's financial markets. It is estimated, for example, that combined Treasury and Federally-assisted borrowing from the public will amount to approximately $60 billion in 1972. This would represent roughly 50 percent of the expected total credit demands in the economy. Only three years ago the comparable statistics were $16 billion and 18 percent.

"The expansion of Federal credit programs has accelerated dramatically in recent years. For example, the special analysis section of the Federal Budget shows that Federal and Federal-assisted credit outstanding amounted to just under $100 billion in fiscal 1961 and to less than $150 billion in fiscal 1967. The budget estimate for the 1973 fiscal year amounts to $580 billion, a very substantial increase, to say the least. The numbers in themselves are perhaps not as important as the fact that this considerable growth involves a massive re-allocation or redistribution of the nation's real and financial resources." In effect, this was a rather belated and muted discovery of the facts of the subversion of the economy. The nature of re-allocation or redistribution of the nation's remaining wealth-capital was indicated in the credit programs. The largest by far was taking over the mortgage market and underwriting housing and home ownership. By 1972 the disastrous course of public housing was indicated by the scandals, malfeasance, wreckage and abandonment of not only older housing but also the newer with ownership of this dead property reverting to the government credit program bureaucracy.

"To some observers the proliferation of Federal credit programs shows signs of turning into an uncontrollable monster, at least to the extent that credit is no longer allocated in the market place but rather by fiat or by political decisions to subsidize specific users of credit. The mortgage market has, of course, been the beneficiary of a political decision to isolate it from the full force of credit market developments, particularly during periods of credit restraint. As a result, in calendar 1972 nearly 60 percent of the total flow of funds into the mortgage market will be directly or indirectly supported by the Federal Government."

There was yet another series of taxation in the offing that was estimated at $300 billion for the 1970s. It was for the restoration of the environment, deteriorated by the heedless, reckless and wasteful use of the water supply, by the fearful pollution of the air, and by the viciousness with which the natural resources had been despoiled and ruined. While a considerable percentage of the cost could be assessed against the industries involved, thereby increasing their costs which would of a certainty be passed along to the market, much of the money would be raised through public financing, governmental appropriations and the like. It would kick up new environmental improvement industries, but it would remain a charge against production costs and add to the inflationary tide.

IX. TAXES – THE CLASSIC TRICK THAT TURNED THE TIDE TO DISASTER

The late Dean Acheson held that he was *Present at the Creation,* meaning the fateful change in American world policy which turned out to be a self-planted time bomb that tore viciously at the economy. Under the pretext of a gathering war, a tax levy of unrestrained proportions was fixed on the economy, and vast monies —trillions—were siphoned off to activate a self-destruct military-industrial economy that destroyed the commodities-economy, the true source of wealth. This latter was reduced to a contracting, involuted economic order, but the parasitic overpower was not relaxed. The tax-fix evolved into many concentric bands, the main fix being for the military-industrial complex. The drain-off of the bulk of taxes for this new economy forced public maintenance works to resort to ever wider areas of taxation. The encircling bands of taxation were fantastically concentric and bled every possible source.

The tax noose tightened on the threshold of the 1970s. The pressure was unrelieved given the conditions of the major booty (taxes) assigned to the military *in perpetuum,* accumulated deficits and the pressure exerted by the civil service municipal groups insisting on getting blood from stones. Where the populace was given the opportunity, they turned down bond and special issues for school financing and in the case of New York State, the two and a half billion dollar proposal for roads and school financing was defeated. The pressure was even greater in those states losing their industries, who were fleeing to lower-taxing states or even decamping the country for foreign low-wage and low-tax havens. By February 1971 state legislatures had before them bills to raise $6.5 billion in new taxes, a fourteen percent increase over the 1970 tax income of $48 billion.

Property owners, especially small homeowners were alarmed at the relentless escalation of local property taxes. Sylvia Porter, syndicated economist, reported that "our total property tax bill hit $37.5 billion in 1970, up thirty-five percent since 1967 alone." In Pennsylvania, a down-spiraling keystone state, leading industrialists and executives were up in arms and loudly articulated their dissatisfaction. At a hearing of the Pennsylvania House Business and Commerce Committee during September 1971, industrialists warned that high taxes were driving industry, commerce and ancillary business from the state.

Smith Kline & French Laboratories, a leading pharmaceutical house, represented by Thomas A. Rauch, president, put it squarely. "As things stand now, SK&F will not even contemplate expanding operations in Pennsylvania. If this current environment continues our next step will be to intensify our studies on how to move additional operations out of the state efficiently and economically." Rauch indicated, a development that was already common knowledge, that many of the leading protesters had already moved, expanded operations and started new plants out of the state. "By any reasonable measure, it is clear that we will have a business exodus in this state if we don't already have one. If things go on as they have, we may soon have a total rout."

H. Robert Sharbaugh of the Sun Oil Company, the Pew family business and leading state industry, held that the taxes were hostile in that they were not competitive with other states. The company had cancelled plans for a $100-million petro-chemicals project at Marcus Hook (near Chester, the main site of the company). Another premier industry, also based in Chester, the Scott Paper Company, revealed that it had expanded plants outside the state, one of which was in nearby Delaware. Pennsylvania was pricing itself out of the industries market taxwise.

The industrialists had earlier, in a full page advertisement in Philadelphia newspapers August 11, 1971, argued that "more jobs will disappear unless something is done about Pennsylvania business taxes. Nobody likes to pull up roots and move away from his home state. That's just as true for business as it is for families. But the tax rate in Pennsylvania is now so high that some businesses don't have much choice. It's a matter of survival. Stay and be taxed out of existence, or curtail further expansion in Pennsylvania and move to a more hospitable state. Whatever happens, Pennsylvania stands to lose thousands of much-needed jobs unless something is done." The signatories were ESB Incorporated (a battery manufactory), General Electric Company, Honeywell, Leeds & Northrup Company, Pennwalt Corporation, Rohm and Haas Company, Rorer-Amchem, Inc., Scott Paper Company, Smith Kline & French Laboratories, Sun Oil Company and Tasty Baking Company.

But the portents indicated further escalation of taxes on the local and state level to keep public utilities, services and health and educational standards running, even if no large outlays were in prospect. Joseph A. Pechman, director of economic studies of the Brookings Institution, the prestigious study organization, urged more sales taxes not exempting food and medicines. He was opposed to selective business or corporation taxes. "State taxes on corporation income affect many fewer taxpayers than the individual income taxes, which accounts for the absence of a great public outcry against the anomalies they produce. Yet the consequences of lack of coordination can be serious for individual companies, which may be subject to unfair tax burdens resulting from different formulas for allocating corporation income among the states. In my opinion, it is silly in this day and age to pretend that the corporation income tax can be administered on a state-by-state basis."

During October 1971 at least four states were wrestling with the problems of overtaking deficits by raising the tax level. In California, Governor Reagan proposed a payroll withholding tax, and there were plans for additional levies on cigarettes, liquor and racetrack betting. Pending was a revision of the system of school revenue based for the most on local property tax. A ruling by the State Supreme Court that the system was not equitable meant that the substitution of a state-wide property tax for this purpose was the alternative. There were also proposals for another spiral of sales taxes and in personal income taxes. In Wisconsin, Governor Patrick Lucey, a Democrat, faced with a need for $11 million additional revenue, opted for greater sharing of state taxes by the cities, opposed by the Republicans. The budget was based on an increased round of taxes on state income taxes, corporate taxes and the usual run of a higher notch on cigarettes and liquor. New York State was faced with raising an additional $1.5 billion and in late 1971 the two parties were sparring for position, fearing to take the onus. In Ohio, the Democratic administration proposed to up personal and corporate income and level off on sales and property taxes. In Minnesota there were proposals to increase the sales tax to four percent, and (what was now a pattern) to levy higher taxes on corporate earnings, cigarettes and liquor.

By early 1972 a temporary but precarious equilibrium had been reached which the Administration professed to see as the advent of a peaceful era. But the maelstrom tides were running swift. If anything, the Administration was laying the basis for a penultimate round of massive taxes to maintain a semblance of order. With a deficit of $50 billion projected for the 1973 Federal budget, the Administration eyed the peoples' savings in insurance (some $35 billion) and in savings banks (some $50 billion) to widen the tax base which would consume half of the Gross National Product—the widest sweep of taxation in all history. Feelers had been sent out late in 1971 for an *ad valorem* tax, that is, a series of taxes on commodities in manufacture.

On the local level where voters had some muscle and had voted down increases in school taxes, a series of court rulings that the method was unconstitutional, threatened to move school taxes out of the reach of the locals.

Joseph R. Slevin, Knight Newspapers business columnist, wrote that the Federal budget "is badly out of kilter. Government spending is soaring. It has more than doubled in the last ten years and it is continuing to grow by leaps and bounds." The tax rebates given to spur a business revival had to be made good. "The preferred Nixon solution is to impose the hotly controversial value added tax, a national sales tax that is being bitterly opposed as a regressive levy, by labor, liberals, and spokesmen for poorer groups in the community."

Seth S. King, reporting from Chicago to *The New York Times* January 30, 1972, on a study of the local Commerce Clearing House, stated that the President's economic stabilization program did not include "any restraints on state or local taxes and these burdens are rising at record rates in almost every part of the nation. The roll-call of tax increases has been awesome. Last fall, thirty states raised their tax rates in some form, as did most of the nation's larger municipalities....So rapid was the rise in tax collections in the fiscal year ended last June that the total take from state levies reached $51.5 billion, a 7.3 per cent increase over the previous fiscal year." The average per capita tax early in 1971 for state and local taxes was $427, with New York state average far ahead at $625, California $559, Wisconsin $509, Massachusetts $497, Illinois $487, Vermont $471, Michigan $456, Connecticut $485, Maryland $482, Delaware $450, and the District of Columbia $517. More taxes were in prospect. "The Bureau of the Census has estimated that state revenues from all sources, including Federal grants, for the fiscal year ending next July should reach $96-billion. The bureau expects more than $102-billion to be spent by the states. The omens from this are clear: it will only be a matter of time, unless inflation ends tomorrow and the economy booms the day after, until another round of tax increases will be needed."

Time for March 13, 1972, had a cover story which began, "Can a nation with a trillion-dollar economy be running out of money? ...the country seems almost to be going broke." The tax chasm was apparently bottomless. The decade of the '70s was to be the decade of growing and bigger deficits despite the record high tax load, forecasting more and steeper taxes, a case of the snake swallowing itself. "Between 1960 and 1970, the tax burden on each American man, woman and child almost doubled, from $711 to $1,384." The slide down threatened a geometric progression of the tax load. "The higher taxes and higher spending have brought little, if any, improvement in public services. In many cases, the nation's streets are dirtier, its mass transit more decrepit, its public hospitals more understaffed, its streets more crime-ridden today than in decades. The knowledge that they are paying more and more for less and less service has bred in many citizens a suspicion that they are being cheated, and has fanned a mood of rebellion. . . .Across the country citizens last year voted down sixty-five per cent of all bond issues proposed to build new schools, hospitals, sewage plants and other facilities versus an average of a thirty per cent turndown rate during the 1960s and a mere eight per cent in 1947....At a time when public officials should be planning to finance the pollution-control, mass-transit and slum-rebuilding programs of the future, they are having to struggle to stretch present revenues to cover immediate spending needs. Increasingly, they are failing."

In their unremitting search for new sources of monies other than taxes, now at the unconscionable level, governmental forces edged slowly and cautiously into official gambling. Gambling was a $50 billion industry, if so parasitic an arrangement could be thus called, and being illegal because of the evangelical cast of the population, was the fief of the gambling entrepreneurs. They were collectively identified as The Syndicate, more locally as the Mafia, and more cozily as the Cosa Nostra. Here was an untapped source of monies for the bottomless pit of governmental expenses. The evangelical fear and horror of gambling was bludgeoned and overridden. As Robert E. Tomasson, *New York Times* reporter wrote: "Legalized gambling seems well on its way to becoming a fact of American life as legislators throughout the country advocate lotteries, horse and dog racing, and even cock fighting as a relatively painless way to get new revenues to stem rising state and local taxes."

The ever-widening demands of a self-consuming society made inevitable the growing concentric circles of taxes. Because of growing public resistance and outright opposition where it could be shown, the new order of taxation was by way of subterfuge and in guise of increased benefits. One such that escaped notice and was seen as a gain, was the action of the 92nd Congress in increasing Social Security payments by 20 percent, to be financed by a payroll tax increase of $7 billion from 5.2 percent to 5.85 percent in 1973 to 6.05 in 1978. Edwin L. Dale Jr., *The New York Times* economics reporter saw it as an increase proportionately far greater "than in any other tax." It "will raise the taxes of working middle-class Americans by $164 in 1973 and another $70 in 1974." With matching funds from the employers it "will bring in an estimated $63.4 billion this calendar year—far more, for example than the corporate tax. For literally millions of workers, Social Security taxes are now larger than Federal income taxes. And they will keep going up, without any further action by Congress."

The bruited "taxpayers revolt" was hardly more than local indignation against minor taxes-added items. Nonetheless there was a groundswell, coming not from the metropolitan centers but rather from outlying sections, reflecting the concern of business organizations and tax-study groups. An editorial in the *Cape May County Gazette* for February 8, 1973 was based on a study of the New Jersey State Chamber of Commerce. "It shows that even at its present level the Federal budget will require $1,594 from every man, woman and child in New Jersey for a total of $11.8 billion as New Jersey's share of the federal tax bill." The $11 billion was a drop in the bucket in U. S. tax-derived expenditures but then it was 5.6 times the $2.1 billion for the cost of the State government in New Jersey, 4.9 times the $2.4 billion of local property taxes levied in 1972 to support all of New Jersey's counties, municipalities and school districts. "Adding federal, state and local tax bills together, New Jersey is expected to produce $16.3 billion this year just to pay for government. This amounts to an average of $2,250 for every man, woman and child in the state. For the average family of four, $9,000 a year is a tremendous bite of any annual income." The editorial writer stated that only by effecting a cutback "can we avoid a complete collapse of the governmental structure that has mushroomed to such horrifying proportions. Unless the people who must pay the taxes revolt and simply refuse to pay unrealistic and confiscatory percentages of their income for government services that are not needed and are admittedly wasteful and unproductive we'll all wind up in bankruptcy."

X. U.S. IN RECEIVERSHIP—PRESIDENT NIXON, THE FLEXIBLE APOCALYPIST, HARDLY THE PROPER RECEIVER

There was a strange and strained air of political unreality in the post-war period, marked by a cataclysmic apocalypse centering on the atom bomb. Predicting Doomsday the apocalypists got the economy going with visions of an American imperium policing a wicked and heathenish world. The greatest outpouring of treasures in all history created a false prosperity. The fusion of such fires was an elaborate self-immolation and the Phoenix out of these fires was a strange economic order never seen on the face of the earth. The elected officials, the business-financial elite, the academic-scientific society would not admit that they were in a fearsome terrain of their own making. The people were as one with them. But underneath all was a malaise brought on by structural social and cultural dislocations and a sense of having been lost in historical time except by the landmarks of the New Society.

There was never public recognition of a crisis, much less an official cognizance. All was heavily screened as peripheral to the leading political issues of the day—in the 1960s it was the war in Vietnam. The economists played along by glossing the bad news and seconding the false optimism of succeeding Administrations. The electors were as one with this self-conspiracy of silence. The pressure under the heavy lid was building up and on August 15, 1971, President Nixon in an *en passant* message blew the scene, as the current cant had it. If anything it was an ukase, since the Congress had not debated and probably knew little of such matters. Government was now by presidential rule, but it fitted well with apocalyptic politics.

At one fell stroke the monetary gold system, the Bretton Woods concord, was sundered, a ten percent surtax clapped on imports, wages and prices frozen. The United States was indeed in bankruptcy and the President declared himself the referee, receiver and court of last resort. There was no outcry, indeed there was public manifestation of relief now that the skeleton in the closet had been disclosed. The admission of momentous defeat was not met with defeatism. The public took it as a policy of economic recovery, but refused to consider the policies had been made for the tragic finale.

The aplomb and briskness with which the Administration hurried to scrap the articles of faith in American imperium and start anew won public approval. There was naivete, touching in one sense but appalling in historic purview, of not assessing the terrors of the past. Treasury Secretary John B. Connally, a Texan wheeler dealer with the sharpness of the breed, demanded of the allies and friends who had made the long fight against world Communism, to do the right thing by our Nell who has borne the burdens and made grisly sacrifices. He demanded that the allies help right the dollar imbalance, shoulder more burdens of the phantom war machine for European defense and permit the United States to recover its trading position in world markets.

The Europeans were struck numb and dumb by the August 15th decree, moreso the ten percent import impost. In a statement September 13, the finance ministers of the European Common Market held "that the fundamental problem is that of reconstructing an international economic and monetary system," an interim measure being the principle of fixed parities and that "international liquidities will continue to be made up of gold and, in growing part of reverse instruments collectively created and managed internationally." The ministers wanted the dollar to be phased out as a reserve currency. A final reorganization would wait pending the realignment of the dollar with other currencies, the first move in this case being a devaluation of the dollar.

It was a critical impasse, with the Administration admitting to a $11-billion deficit (it was $50 billion) for 1971. The devaluation was not long in coming and was an earnest that the creditors pressure at long last was to be met. But the greater attention was on the home front. President Nixon in an address October 7 announced what he termed Phase Two of his New Economic Policy. "Seven weeks ago, I announced a new economic policy to stop the rise in prices, to create new jobs and to protect the American dollar." He declared the wage-price freeze "has been remarkably successful. I am appointing a Price Commission to hold down prices."

LABOR: THE LAST DEFENDER OF THE FAITH

Labor—organized, unorganized and disorganized, the wage-earning ranks who comprise the greater part of the public, the electors, the people of the republic, were the ground for their undoing. The organized and articulate were the praetorian guard of the Cold War, savaging the liberal middle class and in the 1960s turning on the students who saw through the fatal destruct and immolation of the Vietnam War. The most ardent and uncompromising in their anti-communist zeal they were the storm troops who engaged in undermining the industrial order and scotching their bread and butter.

The final phase of the free trade debacle found organized labor still manning the ramparts of free trade, the hall-mark of the anti-communist containment stance. As Professor John P. Windmuller pointed out "in 1966 foreign policy issues and overseas operations overshadowed almost all others that came before the governing bodies of the AFL-CIO." The laborites selected for their sector of the cold war the embattlement of the Communist labor representation in international labor bodies. They sought to nullify the influence of the Communist countries represented in the International Labor Conference in Geneva. "In August, the regular session rejected criticism of labor's Latin American operations and voted a strong endorsement of American policy in Vietnam." Only Walter Reuther, United Automobile Workers president demurred, but his was a personal political stand derived from his family background of early German socialism. The sharpest clash was his lone opposition to the resolution of the AFL-CIO at their December 1965 meeting in San Francisco, which held that "those who would deny our military forces unstinting support are, in effect, aiding the Communist enemies of our country." Reuther termed the resolution as "intemperate, hysterical, jingoistic and unworthy of a policy statement of a free labor movement."

But the cold war laborites came a cropper in leading the anti-communist parade. They did not see the portents of the time and when the economy was undercut, they did not seek the reason but instead clung to their anti-liberal militancy. Such awry zeal caught up with them when domestic industries capitulated to the foreign imports. Their initial protests were feeble and self-abashed. But the mounting tide of imports that threatened them cut into their cold war truculence. By May 1971 the Executive Council of the AFL-CIO asked for protection against foreign competition. "Other major nations have adjusted their policies to benefit their national interests, but the United States had failed to adjust." Belatedly the laborites whimpered that their trusted friends were shipping out in search of cheaper labor and abandoning them. They had no historical explanation nor could they get any from their intellects, mostly economists, for their plight.

THE NEW ECONOMIC POLICY: THE ECONOMICS OF A PURPORTED NEW START

The cosmeticized surface facts were sufficient unto the day opening 1972: the crises leveled off and the receivership to restart the economy had the ostensible support of all. The economists were crowing that the productive engine was back on the track and would be a Cannonball express. All nodded in solemn agreement that 1972 was crucial in backing away from the yawning overall crisis, or failing that, the onrush of the Second Great Depression. Thomas E. Mullaney, financial and business editor of *The New York Times,* underscored the positive thinking, putting down the bears. "What was widely overlooked was that the economy had succeeded in emerging—firmly although not spectacularly— from its fifth recession of the last three decades and proceeded to new heights. Little acclaim was accorded such accomplishments as the first trillion-dollar economy; a continued rise in the number of people at work in to a total of more than 80-million; new records in personal income and consumer spending; broadened Federal programs to combat hunger, expand job opportunities and increase medical care, and a slight moderation in the rate of inflation for the first time in five years." This remarkable euphoria would indicate that the official and the business world's view of the economy was confined to a narrow range of indicators, and not its basic contradictions and underlying chaos and that such indicators were false and misleading.

"The great hopes for 1972 are pinned largely on another boom year for automobiles after record sales of 10.3 million units in the year just past; another strong performance by general retail sales following their ten per cent rise in 1971; a vigorous rebound in steel production and shipments; a second consecutive year of two million new housing starts; a big improvement in business capital spending and inventory accumulation, and modest gains in Government spending and

United States exports." To gain these objectives inflation would be kept tightly checked, consumer confidence maintained, domestic social problems solved and the world peaceful. The Mullaney paradigm indicated how narrowly and tightly the disoriented American economy rested. Confidence had been replaced by pipe dreams.

As a matter of fact the New Economic Policy was cracking up hardly before it started with its initial bureaucratic setup. If inflation was tied to wage increases over 5.5 percent then a runaway inflation was on the books. Through December 1971 there were increases granted under threat of strikes: sixteen percent increase for soft coal miners, a thirty to forty percent increase for railroad signalmen, while longshoremen, aerospace workers held out for increases to forty percent. A widening ripple of strikes, or strike threats centered around demands for increases, the strategic percentage hovering around forty percent. The most demanding and persistent in holding out for thirty percent wage increases were in the services industries, government and the hamstrung military-industrial industries, a deadweight on the struggling commodities industries.

Then there was the crunch of the gold/dollar and deficit payments, some $100 billion dollars in European, Japanese and Arab hands. The Continental Europeans were set to devalue the dollar still further and to phase it out as a reserve currency, creating a new monetary system based on gold and ECC currencies. As for the forfeited Fort Knox gold which the United States persisted as American-owned, the Europeans proposed to nibble at it but would leave it in American hands if they were given a *quid pro quo* in Treasury bills, securities and the like, to recover the accumulative U. S. international payments deficits. As for international trade the European Common Market countries were holding for their advantages which was contested by the American side. William Eberle, American representative for trade negotiations, sought better terms for farm exports. "Unless something is done in agriculture, we simply cannot make further progress in improving our economic relations...our relations are likely to get worse," he declared during November 1971. "It is now time for Europe to act as a good creditor, because America is now a debtor. America now needs Europe to take a role of responsibility for the global economic system, commensurate with its currency strength, its income, and its predominance in world trade." Thus the delusion that the United States would be the overseer and activator of a renewed Europe went down the drain.

If the export drive for recovery was held to be the main drive to lessen the alarming rate of U. S. deficits, it failed despite the unremitting pressures of American representatives. The Europeans were not to be moved by appeals to the old camaraderie and the selflessness of the U. S. in rebuilding Europe. They chose to treat the U. S. as a reckless debtor with presumptive airs and foisting endless deficits on their creditors. Neither did the imports level out as the Administration had hoped, first by the ten percent surcharge and then by negotiated contracts. The domestic importers who now had a big vested interest in the business, maintained the high level of imports.

THE DOLLAR ROUT AND MONETARY ROT

The Europeans—moreso the Common Market conferes—had resigned themselves to the dollar flood by Midsummer 1972. Some 80 billion sloshed back and forth and all that could be seen was more of the flood. Gold had gone aglittering at $70 an ounce and the market indications were that it could crest at $100 before the decade was out, to counter the deficits dollar expected at 100 billion. The creditors would be at their wit's end, only they were given some comfort and hope in allowing to buy Treasury bills and other U. S. securities, and stock of American companies. Nonetheless their fears mounted. The vast onrush could not be stopped by entreaty, threats and deals. It was mounting a world-wide inflationary drive and the European countries most exposed to the gargantuan slush money feared the denouement.

Belgium pushed to put the dollar out and not count it as reserve currency. Professor Andre Vlerick, Belgian finance minister, proposed (July 12, 1972) to colleagues of the European Economic Community, to convert more of their dollar holdings into gold, Special Drawing Rights or into the IMF reserves—a nice trick if they could do it. Gold was out of their reach, SDR was a bookkeeping device and worthless in itself and the IMF would be stuck with the dollars no one wanted. Buy up the U. S.?—some wondered audibly if that was buying a dead horse.

But more immediately the creditors were ready to

face up to several choices in setting out for the September 1972 meeting. As Clyde H. Farnsworth, *New York Times* financial writer abroad, put it, the choices were to float their currencies, hence raising it but killing their competitive edge in trade, or accept the growing avalanche of American dollars "and thereby give the United States unlimited amounts of credit," or to impose control to stop the dollar inflows. "Actually, the dollar is convertible through the market and is spendable against goods and services as well as against financial assets representing claims on real resources of which American markets provide practically unlimited quantities. But it is not convertible into international reserve assets." At a seminar organized by Konstanz University, Konstanz, West Germany, July 1, 1972, for study of prospects of a currency union in Europe, Professor Allan Meltzer of Carnegie-Mellon University of Pittsburgh, urged the dollar holders be bold and buy up the largest American assets including such companies as Xerox and International Business Machines.

The fifth hemorrhage of the dollar during February 1973 indicated an acceleration of the breakdown of the monetary system. The dollars were so much I.O.U's and had value only because it could be used to buy the debtor's assets. At this point it forced a devaluation of 10 percent with gold breaking through to the upper 80s and touching the 90s, which would indicate that the devaluation was not deep enough for the dollar holders. In the offing there loomed yet another large block of deficit financing. As Professor Henry C. Wallich, Yale economist put it: "By 1980, we may be importing something like $20 billion worth of oil annually. Where in our poor deficit-ridden balance of payments is that kind of money coming from?"

There were no ceremonial flags at half mast, the ubiquitous Americans going about the business of running the world were not visible, the atmosphere was business like—when on March 11, 1973 the nine finance ministers of the European Economic Community at Brussels relegated the dollar to a dubious currency. Bonn Germany was now in command, having gained a heavy lead in industrial production, capital investment and exports in 1972. A three percent revaluation upward of the mark was only a token of the supremacy of the leader currency. In the interregnum it was proposed to float the leading currencies directed against the dollar. "The central banks will no longer intervene in the fluctuation margins of the United States Dollar."

Bonn Finance Minister Helmut Schmidt admitted that the Brussels agreement was "the end of Bretton Woods. The dollar has not been convertible for the last one and a half years. Nobody wanted it this way, but the development of the dollar forced it." It meant that the vast hoard of dollars (Europdollars in the context) was to find its own level as a deficit currency. Further deficits would make self-devaluation irreversible.

XI. IN THE MEANTIME BACK AT THE PENTAGON THE M-I COMPLEX DEMANDS ITS ANNUAL LION'S SHARE

Situated on the Potomac flats the octagonal Pentagon was a pastiche of the legendary Ziggaruts of history, astride great promontories commanding their demesne.

The modern Pentagon commanded the tributes of the greatest productive society in history. That this great increment for two decades had been used for more than traditional armaments, arms systems and auxiliaries, indicated that the movement was not outward, as it appeared, but rather an inward one. The great fortress was the nerve-center of a new economic system that used its annual levies to prostrate the traditional order. The faithful were called on each year to give their due to meet the outside enemy. Their monies were used to prostrate the familiar landmarks of an industrial society in the name of a higher technological society.

In its governance, the Pentagon had acquired the wealth of the country while at the same time drafting its young men. The rites of Spring were a call to arms to ward off the presumed Ides of March. For a generation it was duly repeated but the Vietnam War had dulled the shrill tones of the paladins calling from the towers. However the rituals were now bureaucratized and the generals and admirals went through their paces. In the fall of 1971 the litany of alarums were begun with a new range of terrors. The entrails of the buzzard were read for a clue to the designs of the Soviet, the locked-in partner in the charade.

Despite the rising anti-Vietnam War sentiment, the Cold War phalanx were not to be denied their preliminary summons for ever greater efforts. Hugh Sidey in an editorial in *Life* (October 15, 1971) sounded the alarums of the outriders. "In a few months there began in Russia a program of arms build-up and development that, except for a few pauses, has been accelerating for almost a decade. Even as arms limitation talks went on, the Soviet Union has been producing more weapons and at a faster rate than any nation in peacetime history. Years ago, when our advantage was huge, some degree of unilateral disarmament by us sounded vaguely plausible. But now even Senate doves grow silent when shown the Russian figures: 550 Soviet ships on the NATO north flank alone; half again as many land-based ICBMs as we have; a nuclear sub fleet that will be bigger than ours in a couple of years. Pentagon officials say they hesitate to release all the new intelligence on Soviet arms for fear of credibility problems." Secretary of Defense Melvin Laird rose to the occasion as seen in the Pentagon. "Merely to keep up with the Russians, Laird is now planning to seek an increase in defense spending for the next fiscal year, just when everyone else talks of defense cutbacks, reduced taxes and peace dividends."

Joseph Alsop, another intellectual stalwart of the military-industrial complex, was even more solemn. "The point is that a watershed in world affairs has been passed, and a quite new situation has been created because of the enormous increase of Soviet nuclear-strategic power." The Navy added to the cries, bewailing the alleged reduction of United States naval strength *vis-a-vis* the Soviet. The admirals insisted that Soviet naval strength was mounting steadily while American combatant surface ships showed a slide downward on the graph. Another alarmist, Robert C. Moot, Assistant Secretary of Defense (comptroller) held that "the nation is allocating its resources, money and work force to defense at a rate which is half, or less, of the peak during the Korean war and sharply on the decrease since 1968." Moot complained that "non-defense public spending for the past four years has been increasing at a rate of $22 billion a year."

All of which was not lost on President Nixon in his State of the Union message before the joint session of Congress late in January 1971. The defense budget was set at $81 billion as later revealed. In his message the President proposed "a substantial budget increase to preserve the sufficiency of our strategic nuclear deterrent, including an allocation of over $900 million to improve our sea-based deterrent force. . . .Build additional missile launching submarines carrying a new and far more effective missile, replacement of Polaris submarine missiles with the Poseidon missile system, replacing older land-based missiles with Minuteman III. . . $2 billion more for Navy shipbuilding. . .$838 million more for military research and development...more money for new weapons systems for land forces."

The civilian forces inside and outside the complex bestirred themselves. The American Security Council in a letter to its supporters (January 7, 1972) averred there was concern for "our nation's survival. America is no longer the world's first military power. We are second to Russia—and the Communists are widening their lead every week.... Meanwhile our effective military spending has been cut by about twenty-five per cent under the present Administration." Of the growing numbers of Congress calling for arms reduction the Council held that they meant well "but their policies are suicide." The Council proposed "a massive crusade for survival" to get the Congress to maintain and increase the defense budget. If precedent defense budgets were any measure of the monies for the m/i forces, the adopted budget was the floor and new accretions were accumulated during the fiscal year by overt and covert means, not including the costs of the Vietnam War. It could be wagered that the final vouchers going through the comptroller's office were closer to double the given amount.

By 1972 there was evidence that the m/i complex had developed the contradictions of a cul-de-sac economic order and that unless its levies were doubled it would grind down to a halt. The vast industries built on the non-business premise of cost-plus and over-runs had a free hand for two decades, eating up billions and trillions of dollars. Finally the contracting or overboiled goose that was the taxpayer coupled with the inflationary pressure of the millions of employes, caught the big armament builders in a squeeze. The difficulties of the

Lockheed Aircraft Corporation were publicly dramatized during the early 1970s and bailed out by half a billion. There was, however, more to come, causing indignation in and out of government circles, at the failure of even the largest contractors to meet their contracts. In April, 1972 the Grumman Corporation insisted that it needed a half billion over-run and a trimmed specification for its F-14 Navy jet fighter or else it would close its doors. Litton Industries, a conglomerate, wanted half as much more of its billion dollar contract for five assault ships, and an additional $600 million for its seven destroyers contract. The Defense Department had granted over-runs of $35.2 billion in 1971 and $28.2 billion in 1970. The quality and completion rate of the products was only fair to poor and a number of billion dollar programs were abandoned after money had already been spent, some $23 billion.

The military-industrial Directorate had reached a maturation point whereby its economics generated inner contradictions and failures. But, indeed, it was still the largest single vested interest in the nation, with the surviving commodities industry more dependent on it than ever before. The pillar of power, it provided the largest corporations with a steady increment of tax monies, underwriting the means for buying up and consolidating domestic industries and the capital for expansion of its multinational ventures. It was, in addition, the prime mover on the political scene, the Congress being its political manipulative arm. This was illustrated when New York Senator Jacob Javits was successful in diverting a billion dollar contract from a California m/i power to a New York (Long Island) giant.

Withal the Directorate, operating on its own economic base, was caught in the toils. There were clashes with the older normative economic order in regard to costs. This was evident in the 1960s when it was realized that most contractual estimates were merely the floor for final costs. Called overruns, they were blamed on rising labor costs. The collision was dramatized in the case of A. Ernest Fitzgerald, one-time Air Force Deputy Assistant Secretary, who found and publicized overruns of more than two billion dollars on Lockheed's contract for the C-52 military transport plane. He was put down by his service on unstated grounds of having betrayed the group interests and methods of economics.

In the 1970s the Directorate demonstrated that it was immune to national and international law. Presumably the Cold War projection in home and international politics was shelved and a detente with the Soviet Union and East European countries appeared in the offing. Nonetheless, the military-industrial complex maintained its own Cold War version and it was accepted as the law of the land although patently extra-legal. No one questioned or gainsaid the incongruity and divisiveness of the military-industrial complex's steady growth in sharp contrast to the President's ostensible efforts at obtaining new trade agreements and reciprocity with the Eastern Bloc.

Within the military-industrial complex donjon there was a heavy malaise following the years of playing at games of weapons systems and awarding contracts running endlessly into trillions of dollars. A tortuous scholasticism of high technology had trapped its practitioners. The metaphysics of winding through the maze was termed management, purportedly the principles of guidance and direction. This esoteric priesthood was driven by the apocalyptic belief that it had created the final power in world history. During 1969 Thomas P. Cheathem Jr. a senior vice president of the Grumman Corporation felt he had to shake off this pervasive cult and show it to the light of the business world. "The country is too fat at its management and administration levels. Less and less is going into the direct and tangible good— and more and more into the planning, officialdom and rain-dance operations." It belied a sense of loss for the production of the old order.

Now that the economy was on a course of inflation the military-industrial entrepreneurs indicated that they intended to run ahead of the breaking waves. This led to a fearful rise in the budget, primarily in overruns of up to $250 billion. At this juncture there was no evidence that the military-industrial power would be disavowed or cut down. Or the contrary its power would, in fact, increase. There were no signs or intimations of a countervailing power. There was no historical precedent for this strange impasse. The closest foreboding would be as the closing days of the Roman Empire: the year the tax contactors went out and came back with little. The jig was up.

THE LOSS LEADER PERSISTS IN ITS CLAIM AS SAVIOR WHILE INCREMENT GOES DOWN THE DRAIN AND FOREIGN CAPITAL MOVES TO TAKE OVER

It was not until the Kennedy Administration that it

was officially recognized that vast outlays for war material and foreign adventure left a gaping capital void. President Kennedy in his Balance of Payments message to Congress February 6, 1961, admitted "we are initiating through the Department of Commerce, a new program to bring investment opportunities in the United States to the attention of foreign investors in the industrialized countries." Direct foreign investment was at $3.4 billion in 1950 and rose steadily to $11.8 billion at year's end 1969. At that time there were 678 foreign-owned manufacturing plants, factories and other facilities; New York state led with 168, New Jersey 87, Pennsylvania 47, California 32, Illinois 32, Massachusetts 27, South Carolina 23, Ohio 25, North Carolina 17, Michigan 18, Louisiana 15, Texas 16, Connecticut 15, Maryland 10 and the rest were scattered, except in Arkansas, South Dakota, Montana and Idaho.

The Europeans had probably tagged successive Washington Administrations as mad and the U. S. A. hardly a viable society, a fact which was confirmed by a secret working paper (a meaningless term for presumably confidential documents, of which there were millions piling up) of the Organization for Economic Cooperation and Development, one of the Common Market agencies July 1, 1971 (the Europeans had caught on to the American trick of having a superfluity of commissions for reports that could be handled by one man and a good secretary). In this report the United States was downgraded as a capital-poor country unfit for decent company and on a par with what were called the poor or underdeveloped countries. "Medium-Term Trends" prepared for the Zurich gnomes and other monetary long-faces, held that the United States would have to import gobs of capital to keep going. By 1975 she would be in permanent imbalance on the international trade level ever deeper a debtor country with little hope of pulling out. All they could do was shrug their shoulders; it was a case of the disoriented Americans digging their own graves, while under the delusion that they were masters of the world.

But the grave was being dug faster than could be expected by even the most cynical. The international payments deficit was shooting up to dizzying heights and pending the realignment of currencies as a tentative stop-gap, the Europeans were willing to trade some of their vast dollar holdings for Treasury securities. By December 1971 the European banks had a pot of $17.7 billion in such securities and their forbearance had supplied them with this safety valve.

THE TROJAN HORSE WHEEDLED IN BY URGING OF BELEAGUERED U.S.

The *sang froid* of the three Administrations in their repeated assurances that all was well while deficits piled up (by December 1972, $80 billion was held by Europeans, $54 billion by the Japanese and $20 billion by oil-producing Arab countries) was self-deceptive and self-defeating. From behind the closed doors of the Treasury Department, where successive officials were expected to work their magic, the most bewildering schemes, aide de memoirs and placating announcements, emerged without logic or reason. When their backs were finally against the wall, they retreated to the desperate maneuver of declaring bankruptcy: creditors were invited to appropriate part of the going business, through Treasury notes, stock investment, move-ins and takeovers of given U. S. plants. The creditors were also urged to move in for their own manufacture, banking and commerce. By 1970 foreign creditors and investors had established a considerable beachhead in the United States, some $87 billion worth.

If the foreign creditors hesitated in the face of persistent urgings, it was because the European central banks and fiscal authorities did not like the "escape clause." Implicit in the welcome was that the creditors would recognize, if not approve, the wild deficit rampage, by their financing of these dying businesses with their country's credit and monies. In addition, foreign industrialists and corporations were less than enraptured by the possibilities in a deficit country. They felt that they were being taken advantage of by a wily debtor who transferred his debts but refused access to his investments in the more viable countries. It was so strangely unorthodox, so daring and desperate a gamble, that it overwhelmed them by its audacity.

By the opening of the 1970s the creditors entered into the game plan as the business cant had it. Often it was the only choice open to them, for they had lost their faith in the promises of reform of deficit financing, and the stabilization of the international monetary system was even farther away. A new balance had been reached: deficit financing would continue but its expansive push would be delimited. This new phase was not lost on American bankers. A. W. Clausen, president of Bank of America Corporation, the leading consortium of the West Coast, drawing on a study by Judd Polk

("World Companies and New World Economy" for U. S. Council International Chamber of Commerce, March 1971), pointed up the new course. "Probably more than half of international production is done by non-U. S. multinationals; as the entry stakes for the multinational game diminish during the next decade, an increasing number of non-U. S. firms will find that they can afford to play. Over the shorter term, the realignment of currencies will exert a powerful stimulant for non-U. S. multinationals to establish production facilities in the United States, while at the same time inhibiting U. S.-firm expansion abroad." Warning enough: there would be no balanced *quid pro quo,* the foreigners would move in to claim their due while cutting down on the American deficit-financing spiral.

ALL EYES LOOK TO THE RISING SUN OF JAPAN NOW THAT IT HAS SET IN THE UNITED STATES

The new Japan was peculiarly the creation and creature of the United States, the late General Douglas MacArthur, as proconsul, having drawn its military fangs and compelled it to work and virtue. So well had MacArthur done his work that by Summer 1972 the Japanese held $54 billion credits against the United States. The mentor-nation had blown its vast capital stock in arms building and military adventures, a case of not living by the precepts it preached. Japan, *vis-a-vis* the United States, was the major factor in the growing U. S. trade imbalance through the 1960s. The latter was now the supplicant begging Japan to take more imports, requesting that they revalue the yen so as to provide an entering wedge for U. S. exports, and wheedling them to invest in and move in on the States. The U. S. deficits with Japan threatened to continue; there was no evidence that the U. S. had the capacity, will or means to effect a change. The Japanese, if cajoled into using their vast credits to buy into, or buy up, American industries (or such as were around) could, by the late 1980s, have owned the majority of stock of domestic corporations.

As early as Summer 1972 the domestic textile interests in South Carolina and Georgia signalled that they were not averse to a take-over, if in turn they were given a piece of the action in Japanese textiles. Previously, they had sent two missions to lure the Japanese to locate in the South, but the Nipponese, were not, as yet, crying for the Carolinas. The compromise, which the American interests saw as a first phase step, was to buy Japanese textiles. Spring Mills had for some time been importing fabrics from Kyote, and other mills had followed suit.

More menacing to America's future was the interest shown in Japan by the larger machine industries, the automakers and aircraft manufacturers. By the late 1960s the automakers were up to their ankles in the Philippines and Korea when they glimpsed the more alluring prospect of Japanese auto manufacture. General Motors and Chrysler had established a foothold. For the most part, the initial wave was in equity investment, with General Motors reporting 34.2 percent interest in Szuzu Motors and Chrysler 15 percent in Mitsubishi Motors, the latter producing the Chrysler

Colt. Ford, with heavy commitments in the British Isles and on the Continent, did not rise to the Japanese lure until late in 1972. It then proposed a deal with the Honda Motor Company, Ltd., involving sales tie-up and development of a new automobile engine.

The aircraft manufacturers, the craftiest and most aggressive of the military-industrial complex, were not to be denied. Lockheed Aircraft put out feelers, August 1972, to Japanese aircraft makers for the production of its TriStar twin-engine job. Earlier, McDonnell Douglas made overtures to the Japanese for production of its DC-10. But these were second-eschelon outfits of the m/i conglomerate mix. Boeing, the trillion-dollar giant, moved in to size up the Japanese aircraft facilities. They took it from the top, in a round of talks and negotiations with the Japanese Aircraft Industry Deliberation Council, for a joint venture in commercial transport planes. The initial venture, in equal share, was for a 225-passenger job, facilities for which would be geared up by 1973. The Boeing front office was confident of its prospects. "We are pleased with our reported selection by the Japanese to work with them on a possible new aircraft development endeavor. We have had an excellent working relationship with the Japanese airlines and aerospace industries in the past and look forward to an agreement on a memorandum of understanding and to defining details of the cooperative effort." (October 9, 1972). The Japanese, in gratitude for the confidence reposed in them for the new and possibly dominant center of aircraft manufacture, bought four Boeings, a short-range version of its 747, and six Lockheed Tri-Stars.

During this period the Bank of Tokyo, Ltd., with assets of $10.7 billion, moved into New York to open its American operations with assets of $3.6 billion, making it at the outset the 20th largest banking operations in the States.

THF ERSTWHILE ENEMIES ALONE OFFER SUCCOUR TO A FLOUNDERING U.S.

It was readily admitted that no Democratic Administration would dare relax the cold war polarization. The Democrats were foredoomed to show their earnestness by deeds, however historically incongruous, ending in the disaster of the Vietnam War. Only the Republicans, who were the accusers and inciters in the first instance, were accorded more flexibility. Thus President Nixon, paladin of the last ditch evangelicals, could pull off trips to China and the Soviet Union with no formal change in the cold war syndrome. The position taken was that it opened trade possibilities at a juncture when the U.-S. trade balance was growing worse. The putative enemies were receptive. The Soviet Union was in severe crisis after two decades of playing foil to the American war pattern. In their pursuit of the locked-in enmity the Soviets had burned up their capital stock, some 100 trillion rubles, wasted some 50 billion in Mideast adventures and was one with the U.S. in wasting the substance of the earth in chimerical armaments. And in the background, unknown until they chose to reveal it, was the failure of its wheat crop.

The trade rapprochement then was precipitous and on an emergency basis. The billion dollar-plus wheat deal was hurriedly effected, and U. S. trade and business delegations poured into Moscow in quick order. The electronics trade group was the most insistent, desperate for a market now that the Japanese had pushed them into a tight corner, even on home grounds.

Pierre A. Rinfret, president of Rinfret-Boston Associates, economic and financial advisers, and a Presidential consultant, saw Russia and China as the salvation of American economics and agricultural products the new hope of the economic system. "Look at it this way: the United States has an asset that has been suppressed for about 40 years. We have the most prolific and productive (agricultural) system in the world. . . .President Nixon has reopened trade with China and Russia. This trade will depend heavily on agriculture and the capital equipment that produces food. . . .The importance of trade and barter with China and Russia transcends agriculture and has important bearing upon our world trade position." The two super-powers, the United States and Russia, who had pledged their fortune and lives on a final show-down in battle, were now superbankrupts. Rinfret saw the embrace of the two in ecstatic terms. "We have, in my judgment, dealt ourselves a new hand in world trade and done it with a trump card." He was jubilant about the proposed barter trade for Soviet liquefied natural gas, a $45 billion project.

XII. U.S. IN ITS FALL PERSISTS IN DRAGGING WORLD INTO A VAST CRISIS

A world crisis of encompassing proportions was inevitable since the purportedly free countries (principally Western Europe) hitched their fate to the American chariot rushing blindly toward the Sun, and the Communist world, reacting in antiphonal consonance, wasted its wealth in a like manner. The American world experiment—the fantasy incubated in the Truman Administration—shattered the fabric of international law, depleted the monies of all leading countries in monstrous armaments (upward of a half trillion dollars annually for more than a generation), and undermined the United Nations with illegal wars, aiding and abetting the remnants of colonial landlordism.

All grandiose schemes for helping what was termed the underdeveloped or Third World fledgling country nations were now seen as merely cover for a wild growth of militarization, with its expenditure of billions for arms and non-productive uses. The irony was compounded when it developed that the two military-based nations, Germany and Japan, who were held down to insignificant military roles, used their capital for value-added commodities making them leaders in the world markets.

The United Kingdom paid the highest price for its support of American policies, ensconced as a junior partner in the irresponsible adventures for "world peace." The Labor Party administrations moreso than the Conservative failed to recognize that historically, they needed to restore Britain to its former position, if not as an imperial power, at least as the workshop of the world, from which its former eminence flowed. Instead, dragging at the rear of the American careening chariot, it wasted its substance on esoteric weaponry and aircraft systems and neglected and/or bypassed commodity production.

By mid-summer 1971 the (British) National Institute of Economic and Social Research could warn that the economic situation was at a desperation level. Inflation skyrocketed, with higher wages, higher prices, ever-increasing unemployment, fewer exports and the balance of payments edging toward the deficit line without any real prospect for investment money. Then, too, the growth ratio (hardly of commodities) at 2.8 percent was low. Another study indicated that the British economy under American pressure and direction had indeed followed suit and phased out commodity production, so that upon entering the 1970s, sixty percent of the gainfully employed were not productive, that is, engaged in value added commodities in the classic Richardo-Marxian-Marshall school.

On the political-philosophical level, a sense of doom alternated with a naive faith in the rebuilding of the economy by joining the European Economic Community. D. E. Bland and K. W. Watkins in their study, *Can*

Britain Survive? (1971) were concerned with the failure of parliamentary government to close in on the economic and attendant political and moral problems. The political forces failed to reveal the extent to which the United Kingdom had been undermined as a manufacturing and financial power and overseas business entrepot. Monies were spent on arms, aircraft and schemes which maintained a false imperial position. The workship was neglected, let down or phased out, the seedcorn was eaten and destroyed (again on the American model). The authors agreed that "time was getting short" for the much-needed changeover to the reestablishment of the workshop in competition with the new commodity powers, to a cutback on the inflationary comparative high living for austerity, to larger investments in productive work and a cutback of the frills of playing at being a power without a viable economic basis. "Whether such a policy could be pursued within our existing political structure is the crucial question. Failure to do so will lead to an economic breakdown. But an economic breakdown could undermine the political system. This is the contradiction which requires resolution."

The Conservative and Labor political initiative had been exhausted opting for play as a partner of the United States. As Professor Robert Skidelsky, a British historian, in explaining the fatal error in being co-opted in the American orbit as against European independence, saw it: "In pursuit of the will-o'-the-wisp of Anglo-American partnership, the British have succeeded in castrating themselves intellectually, politically and morally; with the added irony that it should have been left to a

Labor Government under Harold Wilson to carry this to its painful conclusion." The only politically viable notion was the Conservative move to enter the European scene. "The idea of European union is alien to British history; yet it today provides the only way for the British to re-enter history."

XIII. BOOM'S END: PROFESSOR WEBB'S PARADIGM OF AMERICAN DESTINY

Overshadowed by the apocalypse of the 1950s and 60s the prophets of doom, predicting annihilation by atomic bomb or another world war, underlay the euphoria of a frenetic prosperity. The two were admixed, and the claimants for attention shifted from doom to the excitements of escalating business, while the scientists' and educators' euphoria of good will and economics matched it. It was Hell or Utopia with the fearful ahead of the hopeful, with an ever-expanding list of pending catastrophies: overpopulation and possible world hunger, depletion of all resources in a final splurge and then the dead calm of collapse. No little was added to the litany by the actual course of development in the collapse of the economy (never admitted and passed off as merely a breakdown). The professional and academic economists saw it as a passing phase, the historians did not attempt a view. Off in London Professor Arnold Toynbee feared the worst and prayed for redemption.

Seemingly there was no handy historical paradigm offering a perspective on the ailing condition of the Republic, with the exception of the Great Frontier thesis developed by the late Professor Walter Prescott

Webb (Texas), perhaps the most significant historical thesis of this century, but ignored and misunderstood by historians, economists and governing officials who had no strain of historicity in their ken. The Webb thesis undercut the notion of ceaseless progress and the permanency of Western industrial civilization, by revealing its historical tenure as a temporary and transient condition. The Great Frontier thesis was simplicity itself. The Western Hemisphere, since its discovery, was the historical basis for the expansion of Europe's frontier, industrialization and coevally the rise of democracy and capitalism as the format of industrial civilization. It had been a 400-year-boom, a veritable windfall which in the process of exploitation, in forced marches, created the United States and the remaining parts of the New World. But by the mid-twentieth century, the limits of the Great Frontier had been reached, for the reckless exploitation of its resources by a prodigious population had reached its apogee. It was the historical terminus; the coming consequences were vast and as yet only indicated. As Webb contended: "If the close of the Great Frontier does mark the end of an age, the modern age, then the institutions designed to function in a society dominated largely by frontier forces will find themselves under severe strain. . . .Western civilization today stands facing a closed frontier, and in this sense it faces a unique situation in modern times. . . .The lights are burning late in the capitals of the Western world where grave men are trying to determine what that future will be." (1951)

The Western Hemisphere was the frontier of Western Europe which was "a cultural center holding within it everything pertaining to Western civilization." The boom, as Webb termed it, was in the exploitation and settlement of the new lands, and dated it "when Columbus returned from his first voyage" and when the last (land) frontier was closed in the United States in the 1890s. Thus Western civilization, the Metropolitan center and the New World were "founded on boom conditions." Now that the frontier was closed there was no point in talking of new frontiers either through science, technology or the like. "If the frontier is gone, we should have the courage and honesty to recognize the fact, cease to cry for what we have lost, and devote our energy to finding solutions to the problems now facing a frontierless society." It was one astounding windfall that set off the modern boom and created the industrial society. "The frontier treasure of gold and silver is the outstanding windfall of all history." (The Spanish conquistadores got that, and other maritime Europeans preyed on them.) The furs "appropriated by the French and English" were a second windfall. "Secondary windfalls were closely related to the land, and while land is productive, it is a stubborn thing and takes its own time in yielding to man's importunities. It was the plantation, the farm, and the ranch cattle industry that furnished important secondary windfalls of the frontier."

THE PROPHECIES OF DOOM: A SENSE OF HISTORICAL REALITIES

Prior to the atomic bomb-Cold War apocalypse there were serious and objective studies and reports of the catastrophic depletion of the basic resources of the

United States. There was no lack of warnings from government agencies and officials. The President's Material Policy Commission in its official study, June 23, 1952, put the issue on public record. *Life* magazine commented on the report: "Some time during the 1940s the United States passed a point of no return. ...We are operating on a deficit basis, in terms of raw materials, and will continue to do so more and more." Earlier reports were of the same tenor. Lyle F. Watts, chief forester of the Forest Service, in his report for 1946 wrote that "the plain fact is that our supply of readily accessible, merchantable standing timber is running low. ...Only eight percent of all private forest lands are receiving good management. On nearly two-thirds cutting practice is poor to destructive." All the big timber stands were depleted. The Northwest was the last of major timber stands and it was going fast. According to Roy A. H. Thompson, "The rest of the country—from the Great Lakes region, whose forests once gave so bounteously, to the Appalachians—has little timber of harvestable size except for scattered patches of hardwoods, inferior pine and spruce, and some hemlock, all eagerly sought by the small sawmills and the pulps and paper companies."

Clinton P. Anderson, former secretary of Agriculture, warned the Oklahoma Save-the-Soil Clinic, Oklahoma City, April 5, 1947, that more than half the nation's farmlands were seriously eroded or leached and that if a thorough-going conservation program was not adopted, the United States would go the way of the ancient nations ruined by mining the land. He said twenty-eight million acres of crop and grazing land were ruined, an additional 775 million acres in poor condition. The conservation program included only fifteen percent of the 460 million acres of arable land.

The depletion of farmland by mining it rather than conserving it and by increasing the use of fertilizers was pointed out in 1959 by Eric Eweson, a biochemist. "The greater the need for chemicals (fertilizers) the more rapid the consumption of humus and consequently soil impoverishment. America's grain surplus is produced in this manner with enormous quantities of chemicals for the largest possible yield per acre. There is no thought of the future and the need to replace rapidly decreasing humus fertility. The present generation is without any doubt witnessing the most severe devastation of agricultural land the world has ever seen, induced by absurd economic thinking, false technology and biological ignorance. What older nations have required centuries to accomplish America is doing in a generation."

Professor George W. Pierson tried to get at the significance of the mystique of the frenzied exploitation of the land without let, in contrast to the European cautiousness and sense of obligation to preserve and pass on the land improved. "As has so often been hinted by puzzled Europeans, the American's relations with nature are neither human or natural. For where the classical tradition had given nature a soul, and even endowed each element with a guardian spirit—a god of the sea or of the winds, a goddess of the earth or of some wood nymph for the trees—to Americans, somehow, nature's elements were merely things and things to be mastered, exploited, manipulated. And where the hunters and tillers of old Europe had painfully worked out a kind of symbiosis, a man-land and crop-game balance of living, we upset the balance. From the first settlements the records of our conquest of the continent became one of destruction and exploitation. Somehow the settlers and their successors, the pioneers, did not really want to live with the land and cultivate its soils or make the most of its natural beauties, but rather slaughtered the wildlife, burned the forests, mined the soil, desecrated the landscape—and moved on."

During the early 1950s the Bureau of Mines warned of the "declining self-sufficiency" of some twenty-five mine products including nitrates, iron ore, petroleum, potash, zinc and copper. This was the factual material backing up the warning given by President Harry S. Truman in his 1947 State of the Union report that the United States was becoming a "have-not" nation in terms of mineral and other natural resources. Averell Harriman, then Secretary of the Treasury, added to the warning in "We Must Import to Live" *(Saturday Evening Post,* May 17, 1947). "How long can we maintain the kind of industrial economy we now have on the basis of the dwindling reserves of minerals and metal we now possess? Through a long list, from bauxite and copper to vanadium and zinc, the richness of the American earth is running out. We must begin to turn to the rest of the world for many of the basic raw materials with which to sustain our technology."

The late Bernard De Voto wrote bitterly of mining as a destructive process that leaves only desert and deserted towns behind it. In this case, De Voto was incensed against the quick exploitation of Western mines and the sorry consequences. "Mining is liquidation. You clean out the deposit, exhaust the lode, and move on. Hundreds of ghost towns in the West, and hundreds of more pathetic towns where a little human life lingers on after economic death, signalize this inexorable fact. You clean up and get out—and you don't give a damn, especially if you are a stockholder in the East. All mining exhausts the deposit. But if it is placer mining, hydraulic mining, or dredging, it also kills the land. Nothing will come of that land again till this geological epoch has run out."

Howard A. Meyerhoff, executive director of the Scientific Manpower Commission, Washington, in reviewing historically the exploitation of the mineral resources of the United States held (1962) "the public attitude toward mineral raw materials seems to have gone full cycle—from the belief in abundance to the fear of scarcity and now to the illusion of plenty. Were this One World, there might be plenty, but only for the immediate future. The long-range outlook is less reassuring. Moreover, this is not One World, nor is it two—West and East. Politically it is undergoing rapid fragmentation. Prior to World War I we could depend upon domestic abundance, with certain seemingly unimportant exceptions. In 1961 abundance is worldwide, not domestic. The difference between 1914 and 1961 is so significant that it should guide national policy."

World resources could hardly be expected to be available to the United States now that all new nations in Asia, Africa and South America count on industrialization to make their mark. The move to limit or bar export of their mineral resources was inevitable, and bound to affect the United States. As Meyerhoff saw it "the current trend toward nationalism and nationalization abroad is disturbing. If it continues, money may not buy what we need. Are we to suffer slow and progressive strangulation for the want of strategic raw materials? The answer to this question is not at hand, but it behooves us to take a critical look at our own resources. The claim of the alarmists that the United States has become a have-not nation is correct only in the sense that we *have not* looked for hidden resources with the equipment now at our command." Meyerhoff told of the intensified drive to fine-tooth the continental geological sources for new sources of minerals ". . . it would be premature to conclude that we have exhausted the mineral-raw material potential of our country, especially as all the metals that have been mined in the course of our history have been extracted from one million acres or less of our terrain."

This was a crucial juncture for the United States. After such a warning the historian dealing with a rational society would suppose that its leaders would tighten its belt and reorganize its economic base for more economical living standards, not waste or spend a cent on non-economic or non-productive activities and cut back the population for survival. Instead—and this was the fateful, perhaps fatal hinge, reported in *The Fateful Subversion of the American Economy,* it veered wildly on a course of the most stupendous and wasteful spending in all history, weakened the productive economy and plunged it into a tailspin. There was madness in that, after being forewarned of the depletion of minerals, the soil and the waters. The nation was driven madly to waste its substance on that penultimate madness, wildcat militarism.

XIV. THE FINAL READ-OUT— THE IMMOLATION OF A SELF-CONSUMING SOCIETY

In the last quarter of 1972 all the guidelines, as the current cant had it, were driven desperately, horrifically and inexorably into the final maze that could only end in the chamber of the Minotaur. The agonies of what was now a self-consuming society (less than twenty-five percent of the work force in production, the classic basis of American industrial society) could only end if the cul-de-sac was designated by:

—A final catastrophic squeeze of the monies of the people, i.e., their savings, equities and insurance. To gain that end, desperate but ingenious schemes by overt and hidden taxation of the $250 billion thus held, would pick the savings of the people bone-clean.

—A catastrophic turn in pricing the remaining industries, the productive core, out of the domestic and foreign markets.

—A cruel cannabilization leading to rapid inflation and the collapse of the monetary system. Simultaneously the precipitate flight of the viable industries to some thirty-one countries other than the United States would mark the final abandonment of the United States, except as a dumping ground for foreign production and capital.

—Inflation, comparable to that of the German Republic in the 1920s and 30s, which would draw the noose tighter and disintegrate the old productive economy.

The dollar-gold crisis, and the international monetary crisis, were engineered and directed while duly obfuscated, explained away with false promises of remedial action. This was because the monetary system came athwart the grand design of subverting the older traditional commodity system for the military-industrial atomic war systems space travel and other exotic destructive nonsense. The Grand Plan as outlined under the Truman Administration called for dumping billions abroad (to save them from or stave off Communism) without regard to the financial irresponsibility involved.

With $100 billion dollars hanging over the monetary system, worthless unless accepted as such, another backbreaking deficit of $29 billion for 1971 threatened to raise the amount to $100 billion by 1973 and no solution in sight. There was no definite proposal made by the Administration except that of going along with the Big Ten nations consortium in salvaging and patching up the monetary system. The various bookkeeping devices were accepted by the Europeans who feared the house would come down if they yanked the American props too quickly. With $75 billion dollars stacked up and in circulation the Europeans also accepted the news that there would be no dollar conversions hereon in. They were engaged in back-door salvage, taking Treasury notes and other securities, but that was hardly more than $20 billion. At the rate by which the American deficit dollars were pouring in they could never hope to recover their money. But what could the Continentals and Japanese do? Pray and hope, that Americans somehow acquired sense, if not honor. They accepted but did not put much faith in Secretary of the Treasury John B. Connally's promise that discussions for "long-range restructuring will begin at the appropriate time this year." Feeling the need to give more assurance he said that the Administration proposed not to forget the problem in "benign neglect" as had previous Administrations. But there was no substance in that promise.

In the wings, the Continentals with the French in the lead, pledged to gold forever, were scheming with all the aplomb and confidence of the Great Creditor to close in on the Greened Giant. It was on a grand design (if a foreclosure may be called that), given yet more determination by the $50 billion U. S. budget deficit for 1971, and the grand total of $100 billion expected in European hands by 1973. An inkling of what was coming was indicated by Julien-Pierre Koszul, a wily, sharp-faced Frenchman, vice-president of the First National City Bank of New York and for a decade, manager of the foreign department of the Bank of France. He was questioned by Clyde H. Farnsworth, economic correspondent of the *New York Times* in Europe (January 21, 1972). Touching on what he termed "the irresponsibility of so-called hot money" Koszul saw a new possibility developing. "Here I see something which could be of huge bearing on the evolution in the next twelve to twenty-four months. I am referring to the much-hoped-for pickup of the American economy. If and when people in the States and outside the States begin to be convinced that the American economy is really picking up for good, and that Wall Street is set for another long upward trend, *huge amounts of capital which have been piling up in what I would call the short-term corner of the Eurodollar market, will go to the States."* In short, the Europeans were ready to buy up distressed American industries.

If the crisis could be reduced to a scenario, in immediate rapport with television audiences surfeit with spy stories, it could be seen as the greatest, most infamous of all conspiracies in history. What a story! At the heart of it would be the Federal Government itself or rather the Presidency, egging on the forces of disintegration, savaging the opposition to one or another of its policies and promoting farcical (but deadly) war games, putting on a show of shoring up the economy and running interference for the Disintegrators.

The Disintegrator forces fell apart when the toughies of labor suddenly realized they were slated for the axe, and tried pathetically to put up opposition. On the mundane level the Presidency through Peter G. Petersen, Assistant to the President for International Economic Affairs, tried to head it off by denouncing a proposed legislation, the Fair Trade and Investment Act of 1972, as inimical to American competitive strength that could lead to serious countermeasure. The Act would require double taxation on income earned by investment abroad, an earnest to stop transfer of technological skills, and a protectionist list to cut back foreign imports to $15 billion annually. The Administration had a simple answer: you guys get the lead out and show productivity like the Japanese and the hard-working Europeans and then you'll be back in psychedelic clover.

The Course of an Historical Self-Destruct

The forces let loose with the ruination of commodity industry, worked havoc with traditional American agriculture. The middle range farmer and those on the subsistence level were uprooted, pushed out of farming and farm ownership by large-capital, land-killing mechanized farming, heavily subsidized by Federal funds. In the three decades from 1940, six million farms were cut by half—three million, some 35,000,000 of the farming population dispossessed or bought out of their holdings, a foreclosure such as not witnessed for any farming or peasant group—and sent scurrying to the dying cities of the North. And the South with its wily court-house Senators (Johnson was one) felt its colored help redundant and sent them packing northward. Dumping twelve million Negroes from a primitive and backwoods environment and Southern to boot, was the final axe on the chosen cities. The migration continues at the rate of 800,000 annually. It has a parallel with the dying years of the Roman Empire, when tens of thousands of peasants and slaves in a foreclosed agriculture fled to Rome. Senator Fred Harris saw it as a corporate invasion of American agriculture. "Government has sided with agri-businessmen, turning its back on the little man who traditionally has been the strength of this country."

Professor Joseph R. Strayer, Princeton historian, delivered the presidential address, "The Fourth and the Fourteenth Centuries," at the annual meeting of the American Historical Association in New York, December 28, 1971, in which he contrasted two pivotal crises, one of decline and the other of higher development. "Every civilization of which we know anything has met at least one, and usually more than one, major crisis in its history. After centuries of relatively calm and continuous development, cracks appear in the value system and the social structure; cracks that are too wide to be spanned by the bridge of tradition and too deep to be filled by the rubble of rejected utopias and patchwork reforms. In such a crisis there are only two possible outcomes—drastic reorganization or even more drastic disorganization. *Our own civilization seems to be in the midst of such a crisis."* By our civilization Strayer meant western civilization.

There had never been such national unity in history as informed the mutual self-destruction of the American economic system marked by its underlying evangelical zeal. In mounting a united war carried to the world at large, the apocalypse had carried it to the homeland, such as it was, undermined its industries, foreclosed on the future of the oncoming generations, sacked its older cities, established a new economic order in the South and Western Coast and moved its still viable industries and businesses to Europe and Asia. But a perverse man-made apocalypse does not make way for the Kingdom of peace and righteousness. Quite contrary, it continued to the overlapping waves of social-economic and political disintegration. The substantive dissolution created a crisis of governance calling into question the form, meaning and substance of government. It established the limits of American evangelical world-view and its disasters in world policy.

A vast chaos underlies American society even if it does not inform it or is recognized. All move across a darkling plain not seeing their condition or not wish-

The Course of an Historical Self-Destruct

ing to recognize it so much as to explain it away. There is an occasional muted cry of despair. Banker Donald C. Platten, chairman of The Chemical Bank, New York: "If we do not begin now to rebuild an efficient international payments mechanism, we can be certain that expansion of world trade and investment will begin grinding to a halt. Should this happen, we might soon see the beginning of world-wide deflation that eventually would make the Great Depression of the 1930s seem like a summer festival." (March 1973)

There had never been economic-social disintegration on such a scale. Professor Toynbee in his paradigms of the rise and fall of some twenty civilizations had not encompassed such factors. The wild money-burning and destruction of commodities production created a frenetic prosperity that scattered prodigious monies as it shattered industry. The connection between the two was not understood and the insistence that prosperity was still active was in fact a persistent delusion.

A BRIEF BIBLIOGRAPHY

Blackburn, Albert W. "Soaring Defense Costs...Blame It on the System," *The New York Times,* April 1, 1973.

Clausen, A. W. "The Internationalized Corporation. An Executive's View," *The Annals of the American Academy of Political and Social Science,* September 1972.

DeVoto, Bernard. "The West Against Itself," *Harper's,* January, 1947.

Freund, William C. "Better, Cheaper Services?", *The New York Times,* June 13, 1971.

Kennedy, John F. "New England and the South—the Struggle for Industry," *Atlantic,* January, 1954.

Lieber, Richard. *America's Natural Wealth: A Story of the Use and Abuse of Our Resources.* Harper & Bros. 1942.

Mansfield, Edwin. "Contribution of R & D to Economic Growth in the United States," *Science,* February 4, 1972.

Meyerhoff, Howard A. "Mineral Raw Materials in the National Economy," *Science,* February 16, 1962.

"No Butz About It—How're Ya Gonna Keep 'Em Down on the Farm?", statement by Senator Fred Harris, *Not Man Apart,* February 1972.

Olds, Irving S. "Inflation or Free Enterprise," *Control or Fate in Economic Affairs.* Proceedings of The Academy of Political Science, Columbia University, New York, 1971.

Olson, Mancur and Clague, Christopher K. "Dissent in Economics: The Convergence of Extremes," *Social Research* (Graduate Faculty, New School for Social Research), Winter, 1971.

Pierson, George W. "A Restless Temper. . .," *The American Historical Review,* July, 1964.

Spengler, Joseph J. "Social Science and the Collectivization of *Hubris." Political Science Quarterly,* March, 1972.

Thompson, Roy A. H. "What's Happening to the Timber," *Harper's,* April, 1945.

Wiles, Peter. "The Necessity and Impossibility of Political Economy," *History and Theory,* Volume XI, Number 1, 1972.

APPENDIX I

Projected Deficits 1973-1979

1. Balance of payments deficits, 1973: $100 billion.
2. Annual deficits, 1973: $10-50 billion; 1979: $70-105 billion.
3. Potential oil import deficits, 1979: $175 billion.

Sale of valuables to gain new assets or redeem deficits.

1. Foreign investment in plant-industry: 1973-1979 $85 billion to $150 billion.
2. Marketable United States securities 1973-1979: $35 billion to $100 billion.
3. Foreign purchase through Stock Exchange 1973-1979: $5 billion annually to $50 billion.

The Disintegrating Money Market

The capital market was disorganized by a wild scramble following the stock market crash of 1970-71 when $375 billion was lost, or acknowledged to be dead capital. The strongest centrifugal pull was by the Government, wasting all about it, seeking endless billions to fill a bottomless pit. The massive Treasury refinancings were given the edge by the highest interest rates (August 1973): 10.50 for Federal funds, 8.486 for

3-month Treasury bills, and 6.90 for long-term Treasury bonds, as against a discount rate of 7 percent, commercial prime rate of 9.25 and 10 percent for commercial paper. Even so Treasury refinancing was suspect since its May 1970 3.5 billion 7¾ percent 18 month notes through its 20-year 7½ percent to yield 8 percent August 1973 fell short and was forced on banks. The prime banks, savings and loan associations and insurance companies were overloaded with Government obligations, now a self-destruct operation, and were desperate to maintain a liquidity that was slipping away from them. Then began the no-holds-barred fight to hold or gain the remaining short-term money market by fiercely escalating interest up to 10-12 percent to hold or gain depositors. There were lemming-like moves from one to another with the bait an ever-rising interest rate. In this scramble the mortgage money market was badly undercut and several states rushed to meet the competition, the New York legislature authorizing a mortgage ceiling of 8 percent August 1973. State bonds were disadvantaged and outside a money reach as in California where the legislature raised bond interest to 7 percent from its traditional 5 percent. The stock market was left isolated with even the glamor issues hardly as attractive as bank rates. DuPont-Walston, Inc., saw it as hopeless when "possibly around October (1973) the cost of funds will become so expensive as to be prohibitive."

APPENDIX II

The Depletion of New England and Middle Atlantic Industries

If a *quid pro quo* trade-off of commodities manufacture for military production was expected, the Northeast section lost out to the South, California and Texas. The decline of the older industries of New England could be traced in the reports and studies of its leading business groups and banks from the 1950s through 1973. The Committee of New England reported in 1954 that the region would have to provide 15,000 new jobs annually to keep pace with the normal growth of its labor force. John F. Kennedy, in his second year as junior Senator from Massachusetts wrote a piece for the *Atlantic* (January, 1954) stressing the need for salvage of the textile industry draining off to the South.

"Since 1946, in Massachusetts alone, 70 textile mills have been liquidated, generally for migration or disposition of their assets to plants in the South or other sections of the country. Besides textiles, there have been moves in the machinery, hosiery, apparel, electrical, paper, chemical and other important industries. Every month of the year some New England manufacturer is approached by public or private southern interests offering various inducements for migration southward. Other manufacturers warn their employees that they must take pay cuts to meet southern competition or face plant liquidations. Such a movement has been going on for more than 25 years in the cotton textile industry. In 1925 New England had 80 per cent of the industry; now it has 20 per cent. Former Governor of Georgia Ellis Arnall and other southerners have freely predicted that the South will also 'capture' the woolen and worsted industry, two thirds of which is still in New England, and large segments of other manufacturing groups." Southern interests, with accrued military-industrial monies, made good their threat.

Under such conditions Massachusetts leveled down. The First National Bank of Boston in its New England Report for August 1972 warned of runaway welfare costs, and held it to be "the destructive cycle." The employed were at the level of 1967 with 100,000 officially unemployed. "Our economy weakens as state government spending grows out of control. As the state takes over an ever-larger portion, the private sector is crushed under the burden of supporting extensive government activities. Then some businesses move to more favorable economic climates in other states, and the support burden on remaining business is increased."

Connecticut alone of the New England states accrued a military-industrial status principally because of its eminence as an arms, machine building and hardware center. The commodities area went down and a number of European companies bought into it or took it over. Rising taxation and competitive stringencies increased dissatisfaction. There was a move out; the Colt Industries (small arms and related commodities) quietly made preparations to leave for foreign parts.

Pennsylvania was the worst hit of the Middle Atlantic states. The collapse of the Penn-Central Railroad was a mortal blow. Industries moved out, old home industries proliferated outside the state. The remaining manufacturers protested endlessly the heavy taxation burden, led by Smith Kline and French Laboratories, an international pharmaceutical concern. During March 1973 Dr. Lewis E. Harris, chairman of the board SKF, organized a last-stand organization, Pennsylvanians for Effective Government.

"It is possible that the Pennsylvania economy will eventually dry up and the state may become an economic disaster area unless Pennsylvania businessmen get organized. Both the Legislature and the Administration in Pennsylvania have simply got to face up to the fact that business here is suffering from burdensome taxation and repressive business legislation. If we go on the way we have been, we'll end up with a jobless state. And nobody wants that. This state is in a precarious situation, from a business point of view. We are losing companies. We are losing jobs. We are losing status as a Commonwealth."

APPENDIX III

Newspapers Threatened by Urban Crisis

Newspapers in the older cities, economically the leading advertising media and hence viable because chargeable to commodity sales, were vitiated by the erosion of the commodity base. The daily press did precious little to indicate or even hint at the momentous events that marked the decline and destruction of the industrial commodities order. If anything they glossed it, hid the salient facts and fostered and abetted the official optimism to match the prosperity of the fearful waste of the nation's wealth. They assisted at governance that was increasingly secretive, furtive and hopelessly contradictory.

In New York where the newspapers had each its own constituency predating the commercial apolitical press, there was a loss of that readership. The mass movement outward of the middle class tripped *The Herald Tribune,* the *World-Telegram* and the Hearst *Morning Journal* and *Daily Mirror.* By the 1970s the remaining papers—*Times, Post* and *Daily News*—had been whipsawed by their craft unions. By contract time (March 1973) the *Times* through its publisher sounded the alarm. In a letter to its 6,000 employees the publisher pleaded growing expenses and lowered profits and indicating that were it not for a list of subsidiary operations, a half dozen Florida papers, a group of magazines, including *Family Circle* and Quadrangle book publishers, the *Times* company would be in the red. There was the implication that back-up money was necessary for the luxury of a daily paper. The publisher mentioned three basic problems: the outward movement of its readership, more competition, intra-trade and television and rising costs of operation.

In Philadelphia the *Inquirer* and *Daily News,* Knight Newspapers, Inc. properties and the *Evening Bulletin,* at one time among the leading top ten papers were in a like dilemma. Not only had the proper bourgeois long deserted the city but 60 percent of its skilled wage earners were scattered in the outlying suburbs and in New Jersey. A constituency that gave some civic viability to the city were the uniformed and un-uniformed civil services, the authority-public transit system and the half-billion dollar public school system. These forces leeched unremittingly on the debt-ridden municipal treasury and income, but gave it some adhesion. The Negro and Caribbean influx which continued unabated hardly paid for their own keep with jobs winding down without let and welfare costs on an upward curve. The newspapers sought to follow their old readership and conceived of themselves as regional (Delaware Valley) dailies. But it was a losing game. The Knight newspapers had a back-up in their chain and public ownership, but the *Bulletin,* a family-owned publication, had to make it on their own.

In Chicago the *Chicago Tribune,* known for its anti-New Deal stridency, was in like manner hard hit by the loss of its old readership. The paper, however, had remarkable back-up resources, *The New York Daily News,* four television and three radio stations, two newsprint plants in Canada and four Florida papers and the usual miscellany of realty and other holdings. Its earnings were a low $13.5 million in 1971 but recovered for a rise to $19.3 million in 1972, and went public in a limited fashion.

INDEX

AFL-CIO Executive Council, asks for protection against imports, 131

Ahlbrandt, Roger S., president of Allegheny Ludlum Industries, Inc., sees need for new strategy in international trade, 44

Alsop, Joseph, columnist, stalwart of the military-industrial complex, 141

American Apparel Manufacturers Association, warns of rapid downtrend in industry, 49

American Security Council, The, demand more arms for "our nation's survival", 142

American Iron and Steel Institute 1971 meeting. William J. Stephens, chairman of Laughlin Steel Corporation, warns of dangers to industry, 43

Anderson, Clinton P., on farmlands, 162

Bethlehem Steel Corporation, closing plants and units, 45, 46, 47

Binzen, Peter H., staff writer (Philadelphia) *Evening Bulletin,* on growth of service industries and loss of productive jobs, 56, 57

Botany Industries, Inc., shows losses, 49

Bland, D.E. and K.W. Watkins *Can Britain Survive?* 156, 157

Burby, John, *The Great American Motion Sickness: Or Why You Can't Get There from Here* (1971), 66

Bureau of Mines, warns of "declining self-sufficiency" in minerals, 164

Burlington Industries, Inc. premier textile firm, lower earnings, 47, closing Southern mills, 48

Burns, Arthur, chairman of Federal Reserve Board, cautiously optimistic, 94

Bush, Dr. Vannevar, president of Carnegie Institution, warns of depletions in retiring report of 1955, 24, 25

Canada, 39

Cape May County Gazette, editorial on tax study by New Jersey State Chamber of Commerce, 125, 126

Casey, Wm. J., chairman of SEC, 111

Caterpillar Company, The. Annual report 1970 hits domestic wage structure, 37, 38, 39

Chase Manhattan Bank, outward moves, 84

Chrysler Corporation, The. tie-up with Japanese, 36

Citibank, economic review of the First National Bank of New York, 93, 94

Clausen, A.W., president of Bank of America Corporation, 148, 149

Collins & Aikman, Donald F. McCullough, chairman, complains, 48

Commerce Department, defends out-

ward mass movement of American industry, 73, 74
Compton, Dr. Karl T., president of M.I.T., warns 1948 graduating class of "our impending danger of catastrophe", 24
Connally, John B., insists allies help U.S. in deficit area, 128, 129, 169
Dale, Edwin L., Jr. *The New York Times* economics-business writer, 71, saw Social Security rates as incremental taxation, 125, sees no answer to inflation, 105
De Voto, Bernard, on the despoilation of mineral resources, 164
Dow Chemical Company, showing a 50-50 ratio of domestic and foreign earnings, 34

Eberle, William, American representative for foreign trade negotiations, 134
Electronics Industries Association, warns of overwhelming imports, 50; *Samson Trends* sees a dying industry, 51
Ernest, Morris L., *Utopia 1976*, 22
European banks form consortium to move in on U.S., 86, 87
Eweson, Eric, on excess working of farmlands, 163

Fabricant, Solomon, professor of economics, New York University, 95
Fateful Subversion of the American Economy Consequent on the Gold/Dollar, Trade/Economic and Tax Crises, The, 20, 42
First National Bank of Boston, warns against crushing private sector, 59; Richard D. Hill, chairman, sees "economic maturity", 63, 64; moves out to national factoring and foreign investments, 84
Fitzgerald, A. Ernest, publicized military-industrial overruns in the billions, 144
Ford, Henry, II, pessimistic about meeting foreign competition, 35; dissatisfaction with American scene, 69, 70
Foldessy, Edward P., *Wall Street Journal* reports on banks foreign earnings, 88
Freeman, Gaylord A., Jr., chairman of First National Bank of Chicago, would put up U.S. industries for sale to dollar holders, 77, 78
Freund, Dr. William C., economist, of the N.Y.S.E. warns against government/service unions, 53, 54
Furnas, Dr. Clifford C., chancellor of the University of Chicago, deplores depleted resources, 25

Galbraith, J.K., *The Affluent Society* mentioned by Green, 26, 92, 93
Gambling, as a form of regressive taxation, 124
General Electric, foreign versus domestic earnings, 34
General Motors, moving in on Japan, 36
Gerstacker, Carl A., chairman of Dow Chemical Company, wants "truly anational corporations", 74, 75
Gimbel Brothers, 81
Goldman, J.E., of Xerox Corporation, defends the non-productive now the greater part of GNP, 58
Gulf and Western Industries, 32

Great Atlantic & Pacific Tea Company, The, 81
Great Depression of 1930s, reference to, 21
Green, Philip, political scientist, doubts validity of national destiny, 26, 27, 28
Grumman Corporation, insists on half-billion overrun, 143; Thomas A. Cheathem, Jr., senior vice president on the unbusinesslike nature of the military industry, 145
Holt, Thomas J., Wall Street super-bear, 110, 111
Homer, Sidney, limited partner of Salomon Brothers, on inflation, 107, 108
Hoadley, Walter E., economist, Bank of America, sees U.S. world position deteriorating, 95, 96
Heldring, Frederick, Vice-president Philadelphia National Bank, my favorite economist, 93
Hartke, Senator Vance, introduced Foreign Trade and Investment Act of 1972, with Representative John Burke, of Massachusetts, 76, 77
Highway Trust Fund, 69
Harriman, Averell, 1947 warning of dwindling resources, 164
Harris, Senator Fred, on agriculture, 171
Heilbroner, Professor Robert L., "The Multinational Corporation and the Nation-State", 31

International Business Machines (IBM), domestic earnings compared to those overseas, 33

Janeway, Eliot, independent economist, 90, 91
Japan, Japanese
signal from U.S. textile interests for reciprocal take-overs, 150; auto manufacturers move into Japan, 150, 151; aircraft makers seek Japanese haven, 151; Japanese moving into the U.S. Mitsubishi Aircraft in Texas, 87
Javits, Senator Jacob, diverts billion plus military contract from California to New York, 143, 144
King, Seth S., on Chicago Commerce Clearing House study of taxes, 122, 123
Kegler, Cyril L., "Modern Times in Cedar Rapids", 82
Kennedy, President John F., Balance of Payments Message, 146; as Senator on New England industries, 179
Keynes, John Maynard, 92; mentioned by Spengler, 97
Kimble, Dr. George T., warning of an economy of scarcity (1952), 25
Knight, Frank, late professor of economics, University of Chicago, compared his fellows to augurs of ancient Rome, 102
Koszul, Julien-Pierre, French-American banker, on using deficits to buy up U.S., 169
Kuznets, Professor Simon, 89; *National Income and Its Composition 1919 to 1930* (1941), 90

Leeds & Northrup Company, 120
Lewis, Arthur D., proposed National-

ization of railroads, 67, 68, 69
Litton Industries, asks overrun payments, 143
Lockheed Aircraft Corporation bailed out, 143; overruns, 144
Luce, Henry C., saw escalating prosperity, 22
Lucey, Governor Patrick, of Wisconsin, on taxes, 121

MacArthur, the late General Douglas, and Japan, 149
Mann, Dr. Maurice, bank economist, at Federal Home Loan Bank symposium, 113, 114, 115
Mansfield, Professor Edwin, sees through R & D funds, 17, 18
Manufacturers Hanover bank doing "big things internationally", 85
McGraw-Hill, warns "American industry is losing the lead", 62, 63
Meyerhoff, Howard A., economist, stresses need to look for new resources, 165, 166
Mezerik, A.G., *The Pursuit of Plenty*, comment on, 23
Mexico, potted with American industries, 39
Mobil Oil Company, 69
Moot, Robert C., an assistant Secretary of Defense, warns of nondefense spending, 141
Morgan Guaranty boasts of long experience in international banking, 84, 85
Morgenthau, Hans J., mentioned by Green, 27
Mullaney, Thomas E., business editor of *The New York Times*, rhapsodizes on the economy, 132, 133

National Cash Register, domestic versus foreign earnings, 34
National Foreign Trade Council, opposes protectionism, 74
National Institute of Economic and Social Research (British), desperate economic situation, 156
Nelson, Robert A., on depleted and worn railroad plant, 67
New Jersey, losing the productive to the non-productive forces, 54, 55
New York Times, The, leading organ of the internationalists, 16, 17; report on overseas operations, 30; savaged the Burke-Hartke Bill as a "disaster" if passed, 79
New York state, loss of economic visibility, 55
New York Stock Exchange, 109
Newspapers in the older cities– (New York) the defunct *Herald Tribune, World-Telegram, Morning Journal, Daily Mirror;* the remaining: *Times, Post* and *Daily News,* 183, 184; (Philadelphia) *Inquirer, Daily News, Evening Bulletin,* 184; *Chicago Tribune,* 185
Nixon, President Richard M., Administration of, official line that economy was booming, 89; Message of August 15, 1971 scotching Bretton Woods accord, 128; State of Union report 1971, holds line for military appropriations, 141, 142

Olds, Irving A., late chairman of board, U.S. Steel denounces economists, 100, 101, 102
Olson, Mancur and Christopher K.

Clague, study "Dissent in Economics: the Convertence of Extremes", 100
Organization for Economic Cooperation and Development (ECC), report "Medium Terms Trends", 146, 147
Paradiso, Louis P., a doubting economist, 95
Perchman, Joseph A., director of economics studies, Brookings Institution, 120
Penn Central railroad, bankruptcy of, 64, 65, 66
Penwalt Corporation, 120
Philadelphia-Chester area, the depletion of its textile industry, 47
Philadelphia National Bank and Girard Bank, plan foreign moves, 85
Pierson, Professor George W., on preserving the land, 163
Pittsburgh, winding down as a production center, 54
Platten, Donald C., chairman of Chemical Bank (New York), forsees coming crisis, 173
Polk, Judd, "World Companies and the New World Economy," study for U.S. Council International Chamber of Commerce, 149
President's Material Policy Commission, June 23, 1952, 162

Rauch, Thomas A., president of Smith Kline and French Laboratories warns against state taxes, 118, 119
Reagan, Governor Ronald, of California, on taxes, 120
Republic Steel Corporation, layoffs and closing sections, 45, 46

Reuther, Walter, president of United Automobile Workers, 130, 131
Rinfret, Pierre A., of Rinfret-Boston Associates, see agriculture new hope of economy, 153
Rohm and Haas Company, 120
Samuelson, Professor Paul, economist, 89
Scott Paper Company, 120
Sears, Paul B., one-time president of the American Association for the Advancement of Science, 23
Sharbaugh, H. Robert, of Sun Oil Company, on state taxes, 119
Sidey, Hugh, in *Life,* sounds alarm and for more armaments, 140
Singer Company, The, 79, 80
Skidelsky, Professor Robert, British historian, 157
Slevin, Joseph R., Knight newspapers business writer, on taxes, 122
Smilen, Kenneth B., and Kenneth Saffian, on loss of liquidity and capital, 108, 109
Smith Kline & French Laboratories, a leading pharmaceutical house, declaims against taxes, 118; Dr. Lewis E. Harris, chairman of the board, opposes state taxes as ruinous, 181
Solo, Professor Robert A., sees failure and collapse of academic socnomics, 103, 104
Sorrentino, Constance, economist, contends 62 percent of labor force in services and other nonproductive industries, 56
Soviet Union (U.S.S.R.), in crisis, with capital stock depleted, 152
Spengler, Professor Joseph J., of

Duke University, faults economists, 97, 98, 99
Standard Oil Company (New Jersey), foreign earnings, 33, 34
Straus, Michael W., *Why Not Survive?*, 23
Strayer, Professor Joseph R., on Civilization and its crises, 171, 172
Stevens & Co., J.O., textile leader shows lowered earnings, 47
Sugarman, Jule M., New York City welfare administrator, on welfare and unemployment, 71, 72
Symposium on "National Purpose" mentioned by Green as the Great Debate, 27

Thompson, Roy A.H., on domestic forests, 162
Time, Board of Economists, in glowing tribute to economy, 96; another line-up to discuss inflation, 106, 107; cover story on taxes, 123, 124
Times Literary Supplement, "The Runaway Leviathan," the overpowering growth of the non-productive in Western industrial society, 57
Tire and rubber industry, B.F. Goodrich Co., Goodyear Tire & Rubber Company, Firestone Tire & Rubber Co., warn employees, 34-35
Toynbee, Professor Arnold, historian, repeats warnings of fall of empires, 173

Truman, President Harry S, 1947 State of Union message, 164
United Automobile Workers, immobile in economic thinking, 36, 37
United Kingdom, wasted its substance as partner of U.S., 156
United States Chamber of Commerce, lines up for move-out; Arch N. Booth, executive vice-president defends multinational companies, 75, 76
United States Steel Corporation, layoffs, 45, 46

Warner, Professor Sam Bass, thesis in study of Philadelphia applicable to country, private preserves to be worked until they are played out, 41, 42
Watts, Lyle F., Forest Service report for 1946, 162
White House Conference on the Industrial World Ahead, 74
Wiles, Peter, of the London School of Economics, lays on academic economics and political economy, 99
Windmuller, Professor John P., on labor's anti-communism, 130
Webb, Professor Walter Prescott, the Great Frontier thesis, 22
Woolworth Company, 80

Youngstown Sheet and Tube Company, closing units, 45